KV-611-667

BRIEF CONTENTS

KEY | = warm | | = hot | | | = hotter
| | | | = sizzling | | | | | = scorching

CONTENTS

* In addition to chapter-specific reading and vocabulary skills, each chapter includes exercises to practice the following skills: previewing, predicting, skimming, scanning, fact-finding, analyzing, guessing meaning from related words and prefixes, guessing meaning from context, critical thinking, and discussion questions.

CONTENTS

* In addition to chapter-specific reading and vocabulary skills, each chapter includes exercises to practice the following skills: previewing, predicting, skimming, scanning, fact-finding, analyzing, guessing meaning from related words and prefixes, guessing meaning from context, critical thinking, and discussion questions.

CONTENTS

* In addition to chapter-specific reading and vocabulary skills, each chapter includes exercises to practice the following skills: previewing, predicting, skimming, scanning, fact-finding, analyzing, guessing meaning from related words and prefixes, guessing meaning from context, critical thinking, and discussion questions.

TO THE TEACHER

In the 30 years that I have been in English language training (ELT), I have despaired of the lack of stimulating reading texts, accompanied by activities written specifically to energize and inspire the mature English learner. Why aren't many reading texts sufficient? Although English language learners may not yet have mastered English syntax, they still have interests beyond the mundane, and they certainly have ample reasoning ability. And while many reading texts are written about subjects of broad appeal, virtually all of them avoid topics that are deemed "too controversial" for the classroom setting. Unfortunately, many of those neglected topics are of great interest and relevance to adult lives. By steering course themes away from controversy, the instructor also steers students away from motivating and stimulating topics.

Hot Topics 3 is different from other reading and discussion texts because it dares to deal with demanding subjects such as *crime* and *religion.* These topics have not been chosen to shock students, but merely to give them a chance to talk about matters that people discuss every day in their first languages. That said, not every topic will be appropriate for every classroom. Some themes such as *the disabled* will probably be acceptable in any classroom. Others such as *mental illness* or *prostitution* might prove problematic in some teaching situations. To assist, each chapter in the Brief Contents is rated by the amount of controversy it is likely to cause. Of course, teachers should read the articles in each chapter carefully and decide if their students would feel comfortable having a discussion on a particular topic. Another way to determine which chapters to use in class might be to have students look through the book and then vote

on specific topics they are interested in reading and discussing. And finally, even though the chapters at the beginning of each book are generally easier than the chapters at the end, the text has been designed so that chapters can be omitted entirely or covered in a different order.

Series Overview

Hot Topics is a three-level reading discussion series written for inquisitive, mature English language learners. Each chapter contains several high-interest readings on a specific controversial and thought-provoking topic. *Hot Topics 3* differs from the preceding two levels in that the majority of readings are authentic or only slightly adapted from sources such as the New York Times, CNN, and the BBC.

Reading Selections

Each level of *Hot Topics* consists of 14 chapters. The readings in *Hot Topics* are crafted to present students with challenging reading material including some vocabulary that one might not expect to find in a pre-college text. The reason for this is twofold. First, it is almost impossible to deal with these "hot" topics in a meaningful way without more sophisticated vocabulary. Second, and more importantly, it is ineffective to teach reading strategies using materials that provide no challenge. In the same way that one would not use a hammer to push in a thumbtack, readers do not need reading strategies when the meaning of a text is evident. Reading strategies are best learned when one *has to* employ them to aid comprehension.

Each chapter in the book is composed of two parts. Part I will contain two or three short readings on a topic. These readings are preceded by activities that help students make guesses about the genre, level, and content of the material, activating student schemata or bases of knowledge before reading the text. The readings are followed by extensive exercises that help students thoroughly analyze the content and the structure of the readings.

Part II consists of a single, more challenging reading. Although more difficult, the readings in Part II have direct topical and lexical connection to the readings in Part I. Research shows that the amount of background knowledge one has on a subject directly affects reading comprehension. Therefore, these readings will move the students to an even higher reading level by building on the concepts, information, and vocabulary that they have acquired in Part I. Complete comprehension of the text will not be expected, however. For some students this will prove a difficult task in itself. However, learning to cope with a less than full understanding is an important reading strategy—probably one of the most useful ones that nonnative readers will learn.

Chapter Outline and Teaching Suggestions

PART I

Preview

This section contains prereading questions, photographs, and activities that introduce the topic and some of the vocabulary. This section is best completed as group work or class discussion.

Predict

In this section, students are directed to look at certain features of the text(s) and then make predictions. These predictions include areas such as content, genre, level of difficulty, and reliability of the information.

Read It

This section is generally composed of two or three readings centered on a particular "hot" topic. In each reading, the topic is approached in a different style, chosen so that students will be able to experience a variety of genres such as newspaper, magazine and Internet articles, interviews, pamphlets, charts, and advertisements. Photographs occasionally serve as prompts to assist comprehension, or to stimulate curiosity and conversation about the topics.

Reading Comprehension

The reading comprehension section is composed of three sections.

• **Check Your Predictions**—Students are asked to evaluate their predicting ability.

• **Check the Facts**—Students answer factual questions. This is meant to be fairly simple and the exercise can be completed individually or in groups.

• **Analyze**—This section will include more sophisticated questions that will have students make inferences, as well as analyze and synthesize the information they have read.

Vocabulary Work

Vocabulary Work has two sections.

• **Guess Meaning from Context**—Exercises highlight probable unknown vocabulary words that students should be able to guess using different types of contextual clues. Some of the most common clues students should be looking for include: internal definitions, *restatement* or synonyms that precede or follow the new word, and examples. However, one of the most powerful ways to guess is to use *real world* knowledge. Students must learn to trust their own ability to make educated guesses about meaning based on their own experience.

- **Guess Meaning from Related Words**—This section focuses on words that can be guessed through morphological analysis. Although morphology is a "context clue," it is so important that it requires a chapter section of its own. The more students learn to recognize related words, the faster their vocabularies will grow. Students who speak languages such as Spanish—a language that has a large number of cognates or words that look similar to their English counterparts—should also be encouraged to use their native language knowledge as well.

Reading Skills

This section focuses on helpful reading skills and strategies, such as identifying cohesive elements, analyzing organization, understanding appositives and elipsis, and identifying the author's purpose.

Discussion

Questions in this section are designed to encourage class or group discussion. For instructors wishing to follow-up the readings with writing responses, it would be helpful for students to first discuss and then write their individual opinions and/or summarize those of their peers. Asking students to summarize is an effective way to examine their understanding of main ideas and themes from a reading.

PART II

Readings in Part II have been chosen so they are more challenging than those in Part I. Students are asked to read only for the most important ideas. The readings are chosen for:

- important ideas stated more than once,
- important ideas not obscured by difficult vocabulary and high-level structures,

- vocabulary from Part I readings,
- and forms of vocabulary words already seen in Part I.

Two activity sections follow the Part II reading. The first consists of questions that will help students gain the skill of identifying essential vocabulary and disregarding vocabulary they can ignore. The second part instructs and examines higher level reading skills such as understanding organization and metaphor.

Idea Exchange

Each chapter ends with a comprehensive discussion activity called Idea Exchange. This activity has two steps.

- **Think about Your Ideas**—This section is a structured exercise that helps students clarify their thoughts before they are asked to speak. By filling out charts, answering questions, or putting items in order, students clarify their ideas on the topic.
- **Talk about Your Ideas**—The language in this activity is directly applicable to the discussion questions in the step above.

CNN® Video Activities

The CNN video news clip activities at the back of the student text are thematically related to each chapter. Activities are designed to recycle themes and vocabulary from each chapter, and to encourage further class discussion and written responses to these real life news items.

A Word on Methodology and Classroom Management

Class Work, Group Work, Pair Work, and Individual Work

One of the most basic questions a teacher must decide before beginning an activity is whether it is best done as class work, group work, or individual work. Each has its place in the language classroom. For some activities, the answer is obvious. Reading should always be an individual activity. Reading aloud to the class can be pronunciation practice for the reader or listening practice for the listeners, but it is not reading for comprehension.

On the other hand, many activities in this text can be done successfully in pairs, groups, or with the entire class working together. If possible, a mix of individual, pair, group, and class work is probably best. For example, two students may work together and then share their work with a larger group that then shares its ideas with the entire class.

Some rules of thumb are:

• Pair work is often most successful in activities that have one right answer. Pairs should be able to check their answers or at least share them with the class.

• Groups work best when one group member records the discussion, so that the group can then report to the class. In this way, everyone gets the maximum benefit.

• Think of yourself as the manager of a whole class activity rather than the focal point. Make sure that students talk to each other, not just to you. For example, you might appoint yourself secretary and write students' ideas on the board as they are talking.

Error Correction

Language errors are bound to occur in discussions at this level. However, the purpose of the discussions in this text is fluency not accuracy.

Therefore, errors should not be dealt with unless they make comprehension difficult or impossible. Make unobtrusive notes about persistent errors that you want to deal with later. In those cases where it is difficult to understand what a student is trying to say, first give the student a chance to clarify. If they cannot do this, restate what you think they are trying to say.

Dictionaries

Frequent dictionary use makes reading a slow, laborious affair. Students should be taught first to try to guess the meaning of a word using context and word form clues before they resort to a dictionary. In addition, although a good learner's English-English dictionary is helpful, bilingual dictionaries should be discouraged as they are often inaccurate. Students should use a dictionary that supplies simple and clear definitions, context sentences, and synonyms. We recommend *Heinle's Newbury House Dictionary with CD-ROM, 4th Edition.*

Finally, thanks to all instructors who, by selecting the *Hot Topics* series, recognize that ESL students are mature learners who have the right to read about unconventional and provocative topics in the news. By offering your students challenging reading topics that encourage curiosity and debate, their ideas and opinions will become essential and fruitful parts of their classroom experience.

CHERYL PAVLIK

ACKNOWLEDGMENTS

As is always the case, this text has been molded by many minds. My sincere thanks to James Brown for believing in the project from the start, then ably defending my ideas to others, while just as eloquently explaining their concerns to me. Thanks to Sherrise Roehr for her enthusiasm and advocacy of this project. I also owe a great debt to Sarah Barnicle, an editor and a friend, who shared my joy at the triumph of the Red Sox and my disappointment as world events didn't unfold the way we'd so hoped. She was a true editorial trifecta—infinitely patient, resolutely upbeat, and unfailingly diplomatic. And to Maryellen Eschmann-Killeen and Tunde Dewey for making certain my ideas became a book.

We also would like to thank the following reviewers:

Chiou-Lan Chern
National Taiwan Normal University, Taipei, Taiwan

C.J. Dalton
Institution Verbatim English, Belo Horizonte, Brazil

Judith Finkelstein
Reseda Community Adult School, Reseda, CA, United States

Patricia Brenner
University of Washington, Seattle, WA, United States

Renee Klosz
Lindsey Hopkins Technical Education Center, Miami, FL, United States

Eric Rosenbaum
BEGIN Managed Programs, New York, NY, United States

PHOTO CREDITS

CHAPTER 1

The Cruelty of Strangers:
Who can you trust?

a.

b.

c.

d.

e.

PREVIEW

As you look at the people above, discuss these questions with your classmates.

1. Which stranger would you ask for help . . .

    if you needed the time? _____

    if you needed directions? _____

    if you needed a ride? _____

    if you didn't have any money? _____

    if you were afraid? _____

2. Can you explain why you made each choice?

PART I

Predict

A. Skim the readings and make predictions.

1. What kind of readings are they?
   a. encyclopedia articles? _____
   b. editorials? _____
   c. personal narratives? _____
   d. news stories? _____

2. Which writer . . .
   a. feels ashamed of his/her actions? _____
   b. feels happy about his/her actions? _____
   c. was afraid? _____
   d. helped a stranger? _____

3. Which story . . .
   a. takes place in a city? _____
   b. happened in the daytime? _____

4. Predict the difficulty of each reading.
   a. Reading 1

   very easy   pretty easy   difficult   very difficult

   b. Reading 2

   very easy   pretty easy   difficult   very difficult

B. Write a question that you think each reading will answer.

Reading 1

_____

Reading 2

_____

Read It

Read the articles and look for the answers to your questions.

READING 1

Who Do You Trust?

by Deborah Hefferon

WASHINGTON—I couldn't take my eyes off the dried blood on his face, on his blue shirt, on his hands. "If you could just lend me eight dollars—that will get me on a bus to my parents," he pleaded.

He was a neatly dressed, young, white male in his twenties. He was obviously distressed yet strangely calm. We were standing in the subway station at midday in summer. The man had approached me as I had stepped off the escalator.

He told me he'd been beaten up and robbed. He had gone to the police and reported the robbery, and now, being really upset, he wanted only to be with his parents. He had no money and needed bus fare.

As soon as I realized that he wanted money, I was suspicious. I kept asking myself questions. Why didn't the police give him money or let him call his parents so they could pick him up? Why hadn't he washed off the blood? That's what bothered me the most.

The lights were blinking on the platform. The train was coming. My questions came more and more quickly. I wanted to do the right thing. His answers didn't satisfy me; his story didn't add up. But if I were in trouble, I would hope someone would help me. Eight dollars wasn't much, but somehow I didn't feel I should give it to him. I don't give money to the homeless man I greet every day on my street corner; I send checks to charitable organizations.

I finally said, "I'm really sorry, but I don't feel comfortable giving you money. I think you should go to the Traveler's Aid at Union Station, five stops from here."

When the train arrived, I ran toward it, afraid that the man would follow me. As I waited at the door, I glanced around and saw that he was looking into space. "Had I done the right thing?" I asked myself as I got into the car.

Later, I phoned my husband and told him about the man. "I really want to know what you think. Do you think I am a bad person? Do you think I should have helped that kid?" My confidence was gone; I pleaded with a child's voice. "No, you're not a bad person. Your natural tendency is always to be helpful, and if your instincts told you not to trust this guy, then I know you did the right thing," my husband reassured me.

For as long as I can remember, I have thought about what it means to be a good person, to do the right thing, to make the right choices. A few days after the subway

The Cruelty of Strangers: Who can you trust?   3

incident, my husband phoned me at work and said, "I'm calling to tell you that you are still a good person and I can prove it. In this morning's newspaper is the story of a scam—a young, white, bloodied man stops women at subway stations and asks for money." I was jubilant; I was redeemed. I had not misread the situation; I had not ignored someone in need.

I speak to my mother every Sunday morning. When I tell her about something that happened during the week, she will sometimes say, "That's so nice. You are such a good person, Debbie." It always surprises me. There is such comfort in those words—in that blessing—for the moment I believe her.

Reprinted from "A Scam Artist or Person in Need?" *Christian Science Monitor* with permission. Copyright © 2000 Deborah Hefferon.

Deborah Hefferon is an independent consultant on international education and cross-cultural training.

 READING 2

Bystanders Just Stand By
by Mike Tidwell

It's midnight at a sandwich shop just outside of Boston. I enter with three of my friends, all of us male, in our late 20s. We go to the counter to order. But something is very wrong. In one corner are four men, also in their 20s. They're drunk and very loud. They make offensive comments to the staff and throw food in the direction of customers. A chill runs down my spine. It's clear. These men want to fight. I look at my three friends. We communicate with our eyes: "If they touch any of us, we all jump in." Then another man enters the shop, alone. He carries a book bag. "Hey, I like your purse," one of the drunk men says to him. It's an insult. Another insult follows, and suddenly two of the men walk over and begin hitting the new man.

This happens right in front of me and my friends—and we do absolutely nothing. We don't move. We are afraid. The beating goes on. An innocent person is being hurt right next to me. I look quickly at the drunk men. They are looking around. They are hoping that we'll join the fight. These are experienced fighters, reckless from drink, violent by nature. Surely they have knives—perhaps guns. The victim is calling for help. I know my inaction is wrong. My cowardice shocks me. I think to myself, "If they endanger his life, we will act." Just then, the shop manager yells that the police are coming. The drunk men kick the man again, then run out the door. The injured man stands and turns to me and my friends. "Why?" he asks. "Why didn't you help me? You just stood there and watched." We look down and say nothing.

All these years later I'm still trying to answer the question. Why? Because at that moment, my fear of being hurt was greater than my desire to help a stranger. For my friends, I would have risked injury, but not for a stranger—unless he was being killed. This explanation isn't sufficient, of course, when I put myself in the victim's shoes.

How could four young men stand by and watch while I'm savagely beaten? The only moral choice was to help. Looking back, I understand why I didn't act, but I've lived with shame all these years, too. If it happens again, I like to think I'll act differently, that I'll be courageous rather than cowardly. But there's a new problem now. My decisions affect more than just me: I have a ten-month-old child. Do I risk leaving him fatherless? My mind says no, no, no—until, again, I place myself as victim. I see myself pleading for assistance, "Please, for my child's sake, help me!"

I have another friend, Myron, who recently knocked a gun from a robber's hand, allowing his four companions to escape unharmed. But Myron was beaten and could have been shot. "I'd do it again," Myron says. "But you never know until it happens." Maybe he would. Maybe he wouldn't. Maybe I would. Maybe I wouldn't. We can't always do what's right. And that's wrong. We can't always know what's right. And there's reason to be sorry.

Reprinted from "To Help or Not to Help," *Christian Science Monitor* with permission. Copyright © 1998 Mike Tidwell. Mike Tidwell is a writer in Takoma Park, Md. His latest book is *Amazon Stranger.*

Reading Comprehension

Check Your Predictions

1. Look back at questions 1–4 in the Predict section. How accurate were your predictions?

Prediction	Not Accurate	Accurate
1		
2		
3a		
3b		
4a		
4b		

2. If you found the answers to your questions, what were they?

Reading 1

_____

Reading 2

_____

Check the Facts

Check (✓) the questions you can answer after reading once. Then go back and look for the answers that you are unsure of.

(READING 1)

_____ 1. Who needed help?

_____ 2. What did he ask for?

_____ 3. Why did he need it?

_____ 4. Did the writer believe him? Why or why not?

_____ 5. Did the writer feel guilty? How do you know?

_____ 6. How did the writer feel about her actions in the end? Why?

_____ 7. What belief is very important to the writer?

(READING 2)

_____ 1. Where did the incident take place?

_____ 2. Who was with the writer?

_____ 3. Who else was there?

_____ 4. What stranger needed help?

_____ 5. Did the writer help? Why or why not?

_____ 6. Why did the fight end?

_____ 7. How does the writer feel about his actions?

_____ 8. Does he believe that he would act differently today? Why or why not?

Analyze

1. In a way, both writers made the same decision. What was it?
2. Compare their reasons. Is either of them justified? Why or why not?

Vocabulary Work

Guess Meaning from Context

1. Look for these words in the readings. Guess the meaning of each word.

Word	Reading	Meaning
pleaded	1	_____
escalator	1	_____
blinking	1	_____
tendency	1	_____
instincts	1	_____
ignored	1	_____
staff	2	_____
reckless	2	_____
savagely	2	_____
companions	2	_____

2. Sometimes if we can guess the approximate meaning of a word, we know enough to continue reading. Decide if each of these words below refers to something good or something bad.

READING 1

distressed _____

jubilant _____

redeemed _____

READING 2

insult _____

shame _____

3. Writers often use *idiomatic* and *descriptive language.* What do these phrases mean?

   a. his story didn't add up _____

   b. A chill runs down my spine. _____

   c. . . . in the victim's shoes _____

Guess Meaning from Related Words

1. Find other forms of these words in the readings.

   suspect   _____

   charity   _____

   offend   _____

   injure   _____

   coward   _____

   assist   _____

2. Work in pairs. Put the words from Exercise 1 in the correct columns. Compare your work with another pair when you are done.

Noun (person)	Noun (thing)	Verb	Adjective	Adverb

3. Look at the meanings of these prefixes and suffixes. Then look for the words that use them and guess their meanings.

Prefix/Suffix	Meaning	Word(s)	Meaning(s)
-er	person who does something	_____	_____
		_____	_____
		_____	_____
mis-	wrong	_____	_____
in-*	not	_____	_____
en-	give	_____	_____

*The prefix in- has multiple meanings. Look for the word where "in" means "not."

Reading Skills

Understanding the Historical Present

Although the present tense is usually used for habitual actions, there is a specialized use called the **historical present.** *The historical present uses the present tense rather than the past to talk about the past.*

1. Which reading uses the historical present?

2. Why do you think the writer chose the present tense? What effect does it have?

Identifying Transition Words

Both Readings 1 and 2 are narratives—that is, they both tell a story. The organization of a narrative is almost always chronological. Writers use adverbs, such as suddenly, *as well as transition words and phrases such as* then, before, *and* as soon as, *to help the reader keep the events in order.*

1. Look back at the readings. Find all the transition words and phrases that tell the main events of the story or anecdote. Compare your list with a partner's list. Do you both agree?

2. The last two paragraphs of Reading 1 and the last three paragraphs of Reading 2 are not part of the main anecdote. What adverbs or transition words signal the change in time? Write them in the space below.

_____

_____

Discussion

1. Would you have acted differently than the writers did in either of these situations? Why or why not?

2. Have you ever asked a stranger for help? What happened?

PART II

This reading is more difficult than the articles in Part I. Read it for the main ideas. Do not worry if you cannot understand everything.

Read It

Read to find the answers to these questions.

1. What kind of study was performed?
2. Who participated in the study?
3. What roles did the participants have?
4. What kind of dress did each group have? Why?
5. Where did most of the study take place?
6. One group had only one rule. What was it?
7. What are some things that made the other group's life difficult?
8. What happened in the end? Why?

 READING

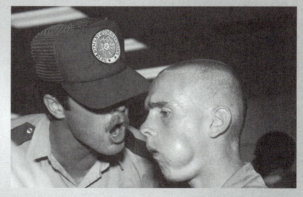

In August, 1971, a social psychologist at Stanford University began a study. Philip Zimbardo's purpose was to investigate the effects of being a prison guard or prisoner. The participants in the study were all volunteers. Seventy-five men responded to a newspaper advertisement offering to pay them $15 a day. All the respondents completed a questionnaire about their family background, physical and mental health, prior work experience, and attitudes toward crime. The researchers chose the 24 most mature and mentally healthy volunteers. They were all white, male, and mostly middle class. None of them knew each other before the study. The researchers randomly decided which ones would be the prisoners and which ones would be the guards.

A "prison" was built in the basement of a building at Stanford University. It contained three small cells (each 6 × 9 ft) with three prisoners to a cell. A small unlit room (2 × 2 × 7 ft) was used as "solitary confinement." All the guards attended an orientation meeting the day before the start of the study. Administrative details were explained, but no one told them how to behave. The only rule was that they were not allowed to use physical punishment. Both groups had uniforms. The purpose of the uniforms was to increase group identity and reduce individuality. Guards wore a plain khaki shirt and trousers. They also had a whistle, a police nightstick (a wooden club), and reflecting sunglasses that made eye contact impossible. The prisoners wore loose-fitting shirts that had an identification number on the front and back, rubber sandals, a hat made from a nylon stocking, and no underwear. They also had a light chain and lock around their ankle. In addition, each prisoner was given a toothbrush, soap, soap dish, towel, and bed linen. They had no personal items.

The "prisoners" were "arrested" at their homes by the local police department. A police officer handcuffed them and searched them—often in front of their neighbors. Then they put them in the back of a police car and drove them to the police station. At the police station, their fingerprints and photographs were taken. Each prisoner was then blindfolded and driven to the "prison." During all of this time, the police officers were formal and serious. They did not inform the participants that this was part of the prison study. At the "prison," the prisoners' clothes were removed and they were sprayed with "insecticide" (really a deodorant spray). Then they had to stand alone and naked in the "yard." Finally, each was given a uniform. The head of the prison read them the rules. They had to memorize them and they were warned to follow them exactly. Guards never called the prisoners by name. They only used their identification numbers.

Every day the participants had three meals, three toilet visits, and two hours for reading or letter writing. They also had daily work assignments. In addition, they were given two visiting periods per week. There were also movie nights and exercise periods. Three times a day guards counted the prisoners. The purpose of the "count" was to make sure that all prisoners were present. The first counts lasted only about ten minutes but as the experiment progressed, they got longer. At the end, some counts lasted for several hours.

The results of the experiment showed that the behavior of the participants was greatly affected by the role they had been given. This effect was actually much greater than the researchers had predicted. As the experiment continued, the guards became more and more verbally and physically aggressive, the prisoners became increasingly depersonalized and several experienced extreme emotional depression, crying, rage, and great anxiety. For this reason, the experiment, which was supposed to run for 14 days, was stopped after only six. Five prisoners had to be released even earlier because of extreme emotional depression. Zimbardo believes that the study demonstrates the powerful effect roles can have on peoples' behavior.

Vocabulary Work

Guess Meaning from Context

1. Do you need to understand all of these words to answer the prereading questions?

participants	responded	blindfolded	orientation	inform
assignments	questionnaire	unlit	memorize	cells
handcuffed	nightstick	respondents	insecticide	individuality
identity	prisoners	solitary confinement	depersonalized	

2. Try to use the following kinds of clues to help you understand the words in Exercise 1. Remember, it is often necessary to put several clues together in order to make a good guess. Write each word below the clue or clues that helped you understand it.

    It looks like a word I know and/or I understood the prefix or suffix.

    _____

    I used my knowledge of police procedure and prisons.

    _____

    I used my knowledge of psychology.

    _____

    I used logic.

    _____

    The writer gave a definition or explanation.

    _____

3. Sometimes you can guess the approximate meaning of a word that is part of a list if you know some of the words in the list. Do the <u>underlined</u> words probably refer to good things or bad things? How do you know?

    ". . . several experienced extreme emotional <u>depression</u>, crying, <u>rage</u>, and great <u>anxiety</u>."

Reading Skills

Identifying the Author's Purpose

1. Which category best describes the reading? Why?

persuasion	narration	description	instruction

2. Give the reading a title and subtitle that will help future readers understand what the reading is about.

    Title: _____

    Subtitle: _____

Idea Exchange

Think about Your Ideas

1. Look at the situations. Check (✓) the boxes.

Would you . . .	I have done this.	I would probably do this.	I might do this.	I would probably not do this.
give money to a beggar?				
pick up a hitchhiker?				
buy a stranger a meal and eat it with him/her?				
give directions to a stranger on the street?				
stop to help at a traffic accident?				
chase after a purse snatcher on the street?				
offer help to a stranger without being asked?				
stop two strangers who were fighting?				
come to the defense of a stranger who was being verbally harassed or intimidated?				
help a stranger who was struggling to carry something heavy?				
ignore corruption at your job or at your school?				

2. Think about specific examples for each action you have done.

Talk about Your Ideas

Use the information from the chart to answer these questions.

1. What, if any, obligations do we have toward strangers?
2. Have you ever asked for help from a stranger and been refused? What happened? How did you feel?
3. Police officers, soldiers and prison guards are sometimes accused of misusing positions of power. Given Zimbardo's conclusions, can this abuse be eliminated? If so, how? If no, why not?

For CNN video activities about work-from-home scams, turn to page 191.

CHAPTER ❷

CRIME AND PUNISHMENT: JUSTICE FOR ALL?

PREVIEW

Discuss these questions with your classmates.

1. Check (✓) the statements you think are true about the system of justice in your country.

   _____ a. It isn't perfect, but it's mostly fair.

   _____ b. Many innocent people are sent to jail.

   _____ c. Rich and powerful people are rarely punished.

   _____ d. Many guilty people are set free.

   _____ e. The system is too strict.

2. Explain the reasons for your answers.

PART I

Predict

A. Skim the readings and make predictions.

1. Which article is from a newspaper? How do you know?
2. Look at the titles of the readings. How are the topics the same? How are they different?
3. What is the relationship between Readings 1A and 1B?
4. Guess why the man in Reading 1 was released from prison.
5. Predict why the man in Reading 2 was released from prison.
6. Predict the difficulty of each reading:

   a. Reading 1A

   very easy   pretty easy   difficult   very difficult

   b. Reading 1B

   very easy   pretty easy   difficult   very difficult

   c. Reading 2

   very easy   pretty easy   difficult   very difficult

B. Write a question that you think each article will answer.

Reading 1A

_____

Reading 1B

_____

Reading 2

_____

Read It

Read the articles and look for the answers to your questions.

READING 1A

DNA Evidence Exonerates Brandon Moon

Texas man spent 17 years in prison for a crime he didn't commit.

EL PASO, Texas (AP)—On the morning of April 27, 1987, someone broke into the home of a woman in El Paso, Texas, and raped her. On the day after the attack, the victim went to the police station and helped police create a drawing of her attacker. The next day, she looked at photographs and said that Brandon Moon, a 23-year-old college student, looked like her attacker but that she couldn't be sure.

Police arrested Moon on May 1, 1987. On May 2, 1987, the victim identified Moon in a lineup. Moon was the only person in both the photographic and lineup procedures. Two other women were also contacted by the police to make an identification. These women had also been attacked in a similar way. Both women identified Moon as their assailant.

Moon's trial began in December 1987. The defense claimed that Moon was misidentified. His lawyers argued that hairs found at the scene could not be Moon's. Moon testified that he was on his college campus at the time of the crime. The crime occurred at about 9:00 A.M. In her testimony, Moon's girlfriend said that she had phoned him less than an hour before nine and had met him shortly after 9:15 A.M. As Moon had no car, the defense argued that Moon could not have been the rapist.

One of the other victims who had identified Moon also testified against him. Both crimes were similar enough to point to the same assailant. The jury convicted Moon and he was sentenced to 75 years in prison.

Throughout his years behind bars, Moon maintained his innocence. Finally, in 2002, the Innocence Project took his case. In 2004, DNA testing not available in 1987 showed that Moon was not the attacker. In December of that year, Brandon Moon was exonerated and released from prison. His was the 154th postconviction DNA exoneration in the United States, and the 13th in 2004.

Jaime Esparza, district attorney for El Paso County, apologized to Moon for his wrongful conviction, "My office and the state of Texas, in the interest of truth, recognize the injustice Mr. Moon has suffered." Moon, who accepted the apology, may receive compensation from the state of up to $25,000 for every year of his imprisonment. Lawyer Barry Scheck, Innocence Project co-director, remarked, "This is also a classic case where faulty eyewitness identification procedures implicated the wrong man."

Adapted from "Brandon Moon" with permission. Copyright © 2005 Innocence Project

READING 1B

About the Innocence Project

The Innocence Project at the Benjamin N. Cardozo School of Law is a nonprofit legal clinic. The Project only takes cases where postconviction DNA testing of evidence shows convincing proof of innocence. Most of their clients are poor. The only hope they have is that biological evidence from the crime scene has not been destroyed and can be tested. Thousands of inmates are on the Project's waiting list.

DNA testing has provided scientific proof that wrongful convictions are not rare events. In fact, it seems likely that there are many innocent people in prison. In addition to helping those currently in prison, researchers at the Innocence Project are studying the causes of unjust imprisonment. They work with legislators and police, conduct research and training, and propose solutions to prevent wrongful convictions in the future.

READING 2

Convicted Killer Freed after Four Decades in Prison

On a rainy night in 1961, Wilbert Rideau, a 19-year-old black janitor, killed Julia Ferguson, a white bank teller, in the town of Lake Charles, Louisiana. At the time, Rideau was practically illiterate. Lake Charles was a segregated southern town. Rideau confessed to the crime. He was convicted and sentenced to death three times by all-white, all-male juries. Each time, however, the death penalty was overturned by higher courts.

During the 44 years that he spent in prison, Rideau became a talented, self-educated writer. He made *The Angolite*, a literary prison magazine, into a nationally acclaimed magazine dealing with the criminal justice system. He also co-directed *The Farm*, a documentary film that was nominated for an Oscar in 1999. He also wrote and narrated an award-winning radio documentary.

(Continued on next page)

In 2004, Rideau was retried for this murder for the fourth and last time. His lawyers claimed that he was guilty of manslaughter rather than murder. Murder requires planning; manslaughter does not. The defense said that Rideau had panicked after a botched bank robbery and then stabbed Ferguson without thinking. They also said that it was impossible for Rideau to receive a fair trial in 1967 because of the town's climate of racial hatred. The jury of seven whites and four African-Americans agreed. Consequently, they convicted him of manslaughter rather than first-degree murder. The court then ordered Rideau released because he had already served more than the maximum of 25 years for a manslaughter conviction.

Many of the town's black citizens, as well as some white citizens, point out that Rideau served longer than any white man convicted of murder in Louisiana history. When he was released, Rideau said, "I think I'm basically a good guy, a decent person. Yes, I did something bad but a lifetime ago. The jury said I did not murder anybody. It was an act of manslaughter and there is a distinct difference between the two."

Reading Comprehension

Check Your Predictions

1. Look back at questions 1–6 in the Predict section. How accurate were your predictions?

Prediction	Not Accurate	Accurate
1		
2		
3		
4		
5		
6a		
6b		
6c		

2. If you found the answers to your questions, what were they?

Reading 1A _____

Reading 1B _____

Reading 2 _____

Check the Facts

Check (✓) the questions you can answer after reading once. Then go back and look for the answers that you are unsure of. Write T for *true*, F for *false*, or NS for *not sure*.

READING 1A

_____ 1. Brandon Moon knew the woman who was attacked.

_____ 2. Three women identified Brandon Moon.

_____ 3. The jury decided that Moon was guilty.

_____ 4. Moon spent 75 years in prison.

_____ 5. The Innocence Project took Moon's case.

_____ 6. DNA evidence showed that Moon was not guilty.

_____ 7. The state of Texas spent $25,000 a year to keep Moon in prison.

_____ 8. The eyewitnesses in Moon's trial lied.

READING 1B

_____ 1. It costs a lot of money to benefit from the Innocence Project.

_____ 2. The Innocence Project only takes cases after people are in prison.

_____ 3. DNA evidence is biological evidence.

_____ 4. The Innocence Project is rarely successful.

READING 2

_____ 1. No one knows who killed Julia Ferguson.

_____ 2. Wilbert Rideau was a college student at the time of the crime.

_____ 3. Rideau told police that he was a murderer.

_____ 4. Rideau had four trials.

_____ 5. Four juries sentenced him to death.

_____ 6. Rideau educated himself in prison.

_____ 7. He acted in a film about prisons.

_____ 8. The last jury decided that Rideau was innocent.

_____ 9. Rideau was sentenced to 25 years in prison.

Analyze

Answer these questions. Give reasons for your answers.

1. Would the Innocence Project have taken Wilbert Rideau's case? Why or why not?

2. Was Wilbert Rideau probably convicted of murder or manslaughter in 1961? Why do you think so?

Vocabulary Work

Guess Meaning from Context

Studies show that you will understand more if you continue reading than if you stop to look up unknown words in the dictionary. Therefore, it is very important to learn to guess the meaning of new words. You may not be able to guess the exact meaning, but you can often figure out the approximate meaning of the unknown word.

There are a number of different kinds of strategies that we use to guess meanings. Often we use a combination of strategies. Two of the most important strategies are **using your world knowledge** *and* **guessing what meaning makes logical sense** *in the sentence.*

1. Look for these words in Readings 1A & 1B. Use your *world knowledge* of the criminal justice system and *guess meanings* using logic.

Word	Meaning
DNA	_____
raped	_____
sentenced	_____
exonerated	_____
testified	_____
assailant	_____
compensation	_____
evidence	_____
inmates	_____

*Another important strategy for dealing with unknown words is to identify which are not relevant to the text and to just **skip** them. Many times you can understand main points of a text without understanding every word.*

2. Look at the following words from Reading 2. Which ones are important? Which ones can you *skip*?

Word	Probably can skip	Probably can't skip
illiterate	_____	_____
segregated	_____	_____
panicked	_____	_____
botched	_____	_____
stabbed	_____	_____
manslaughter	_____	_____

Guess Meaning from Related Words

Another very important vocabulary strategy is to relate new words to words that you already know.

1. Underline the common words in these compound words and phrases. Guess their meanings.

Word	Reading	Meaning
lineup	1A	_____
wrongful	1A	_____
overturned	2	_____
self-educated	2	_____

Sometimes we can recognize that new words are simply other forms of words that we already know.

2. What other forms of these words are you familiar with?

Reading 2

racial   _____

hatred   _____

HH LEARNING CENTRE
HARROW COLLEGE

Often within a reading, you will find different forms of the same word, varying by an added suffix. For example, you may find the verb convict *and the noun* conviction. *The suffix change often indicates a different part of speech or grammar usage.*

3. Find other forms of these words in Reading 1A.

    ### Reading 1A

    identify   _____

    photographic   _____

    testified   _____

    raped   _____

    attack   _____

    innocence   _____

4. Work in pairs. Put all of the words from Exercise 3 in the correct columns. Compare your work with another pair when you are done.

Noun (person)	Noun (thing)	Verb	Adjective	Adverb

Some words' meanings are changed by prefixes—for example, happy *and* unhappy. *In these cases, it is often useful to learn the meaning of common prefixes. It will help you guess the meaning of the words.*

5. Look at the meanings of these prefixes. Then look for the words that use them in the readings and guess their meanings.

Prefix	Meaning	Word(s)
un-	no or not	_____
non-	no or not	_____
in-	no or not	_____
post-	after	_____
mis-	wrong	_____
re-	again	_____

Reading Skills

Understanding Appositives

Writers often use **appositives** *to identify or describe a person or a place. For example, instead of using two sentences, the writer might choose to combine the information. Compare the two examples.*

Example 1

The next day, she looked at photographs and said that Brandon Moon looked like her attacker but that she couldn't be sure. Brandon Moon was a 23-year-old college student.

Example 2

The next day, she looked at photographs and said that Brandon Moon, a 23-year-old college student, looked like the man but that she couldn't be sure.

You can recognize an appositive because it is often set off with commas. The information in an appositive is not always necessary in the sentence. It simply gives more information. So, if you can't understand the appositive, you can leave it out.

Underline *the appositives in these sentences.*

1. Jaime Esparza, district attorney for El Paso County, apologized to Moon for his wrongful conviction.

2. Lawyer Barry Scheck, Innocence Project co-director, remarked, "This is also a classic case where faulty eyewitness identification procedures implicated the wrong man."

3. On a rainy night in 1961, Wilbert Rideau, a 19-year-old black janitor, killed Julia Ferguson, a white bank teller, in the town of Lake Charles, Louisiana.

4. He made *The Angolite,* a literary prison magazine, into a nationally acclaimed magazine dealing with the criminal justice system. He also co-directed *The Farm,* a documentary film that was nominated for an Oscar in 1999.

Discussion

1. Do you think that Brandon Moon should receive money from the state? If so, how much should he receive?

2. Do you agree with the court's final decision in the Wilbert Rideau case? Why or why not?

PART II

This reading is more difficult than the articles in Part I. Read it for the main ideas. Do not worry if you cannot understand everything.

Read It

Read to find the answers to these questions.

1. What numbers does the title refer to?

2. What did Virginia want to do with its prisons?

3. What did researchers do to create a new system?

4. What do the numbers *71* and *38* represent?

5. Which of these factors are important in the scale?
   - age
   - intelligence
   - employment
   - marriage
   - children

Punishment by the Numbers

For decades, criminologists have tried to predict what type of person is most likely to commit crimes and which convicted criminals are most likely to return to a life of crime after prison. Until now, these "predictions" were wrong as often as they were right. However, today the state of Virginia is using statistics to figure out who to send to prison and how long they should stay there.

Statisticians are using numbers the same way insurance agents do—to predict the likelihood of an event based on a short list of factors. For example, if a young, jobless man is convicted of shoplifting, the state is more likely to recommend prison time for him than for a middle-aged, employed woman who commits the same crime. Why? Because statistics show that the woman is far less likely to commit the crime again.

Judges in Virginia are using these predictive measures to decide on sentences for nonviolent crimes. Why did they turn to statistics? Virginia's prison population was growing two times faster than the national average. Legislators wanted to stop spending money building new prisons. If they could figure out whom they could release, they could reduce their prison population.

Researchers spent a lot of time creating the system. First, they studied 1,500 criminals for three years after their release from prison. They found that men were 55 percent more likely to be rearrested than women, and that offenders in their 20s were a much higher risk than those older than 40. Those without jobs were also a higher risk. Those who weren't married were, too.

The criminologists then used their findings to create a 71-point scale. If a defendant scores 38 points or less, he or she doesn't have to go to prison. Instead, the criminal will receive a nonprison punishment such as a fine or house arrest. They tested their model on prisoners who had been released five years earlier. They found that the prisoners' scores correctly predicted who would commit a crime again 75 percent of the time. Only 12 percent of those who scored less than 35 committed new crimes, while 38 percent who scored higher were reconvicted. Meanwhile, the state's prison population has stopped growing.

However, not everyone is happy with the new system. Skeptics ask why a married woman in her 40s who sells drugs should receive a lesser sentence than a single man in his 20s. In fact, according to the risk scale, unemployed single men in their 20s start with a score of 36 points before their crime has even been committed. "If you're punishing people because of a bunch of factors that have nothing to do with blame, well, you're not in the business of doing justice anymore," said Paul Robinson, a law professor at the University of Pennsylvania. Economists also point out that there is another problem. The system might actually encourage people with low scores to commit crimes. Virginia defends itself by pointing out that judges can ignore the scale. It seems clear that the system is imperfect but not irrational.

Vocabulary Work

Guess Meaning from Context

Do you need to understand all of these words to answer the prereading questions? Cross out (~~word~~) the words that you can ignore. <u>Underline</u> the words you already know. (Circle) the words you need to guess.

jobless   likelihood   lesser   justice   criminologist

non-violent   reconvicted   rearrested   predictive

Guess the meaning of the words you circled. What clues did you use?

_____ It looks like a word I know.

_____ I used my knowledge of the world.

_____ There is a definition or a synonym in the reading.

_____ I guessed from an example.

_____ I understood the prefix.

Reading Skills

Finding Referents

When you read, it is very important to keep track of pronouns and to be aware of what they refer to. The same pronouns are often used and reused, but they refer to many different nouns.

Look at the pronouns below. What does each one refer to?

1. Until now, these "predictions" were wrong as often as <u>they</u> were right.

2. However, today the state of Virginia is using statistics to figure out who to send to prison and how long <u>they</u> should stay there.

3. Why did <u>they</u> turn to statistics?

4. If <u>they</u> could figure out whom they could release, <u>they</u> could reduce their prison population.

5. First, <u>they</u> studied the 1,500 criminals for three years after their release from prison.

6. <u>They</u> tested their model on prisoners who had been released five years earlier.

7. <u>Those</u> without jobs were also a higher risk. <u>Those</u> who weren't married were, too.

Idea Exchange

Think about Your Ideas

1. Think about these questions again. Check (✓) the statements you think are true about the system of justice in your country.

    _____ a. It isn't perfect, but it's mostly fair.

    _____ b. Many innocent people are sent to jail.

    _____ c. Rich and powerful people are rarely punished.

    _____ d. Many guilty people are set free.

    _____ e. The system is too strict.

2. Which of these items do you feel should be part of the justice system?
    *   Parole (giving convicts time off for good behavior)
    *   Use of DNA evidence
    *   Retrials
    *   Trial by jury
    *   Use of statistics to decide on sentences for the guilty
    *   Differentiating between manslaughter and murder

Talk about Your Ideas

In what ways, if any, do you think the system of justice in your country should be changed? Why?

Topics to think about during your discussion:
*   the creation of juries
*   the right to a lawyer
*   sentences or punishments
*   types of evidence that are allowed
*   parole
*   the appointment of judges

For CNN video activities about reversed convictions as a result of DNA evidence, turn to page 192.

CHAPTER ❸

Fertility Now:
Babies by
design

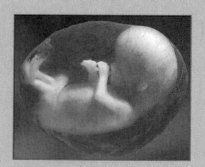
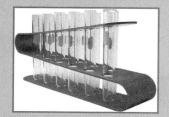
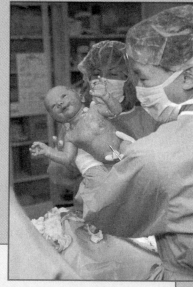

PREVIEW

1. Check (✓) the columns.

How important is raising children to . . .	Extremely important	Very important	Important	Not important	No opinion
your society?					
your family?					
you?					

2. Check (✓) the columns.

How important is having your own biological children to . . .	Extremely important	Very important	Important	Not important	No opinion
your society?					
your family?					
you?					

3. What do you know about fertility clinics? What do they do? What procedures do they use?

PART I

Predict

A. Skim the three readings and make predictions.

1. Which readings probably . . .
   a. give an opinion?
   b. just give information?
2. Which readings . . .
   a. give real-life examples?
   b. use statistics?
   c. give a warning?
3. Which reading will probably be the most difficult?
4. Predict the difficulty of each reading.
   a. Reading 1

   very easy   pretty easy   difficult   very difficult

   b. Reading 2

   very easy   pretty easy   difficult   very difficult

   c. Reading 3

   very easy   pretty easy   difficult   very difficult

B. Write a question that you think each reading will answer.

Reading 1

_____

Reading 2

_____

Reading 3

_____

Read It

Read the articles and look for the answers to your questions.

Do You Think You'd Like to Donate an Egg? Read On!

In March, 1999, this advertisement appeared in student newspapers of Harvard, Princeton, the University of Pennsylvania, and Yale:

Help our dream come true. A loving, caring couple seeking egg donor. Candidates should be intelligent, athletic, blonde, at least 5'10", have a 1400+ SAT score, and have no major family medical problems. $50,000.

Fifty thousand dollars for donating an egg? The best male candidates only get a couple of hundred dollars for donating hundreds of thousands of sperm. Why are eggs so much more valuable? Men have an unlimited amount of sperm, and they are very easy to donate. Women only have a limited number of eggs (several hundred), and in order to donate the eggs, the woman must undergo surgery.

Of course, $50,000 is an unusually high fee. The normal fee varies from $5,000 to $15,000. In fact, the couple that placed the ad received quite a lot of criticism. People complained that they were elitist because they insisted on a donor from an Ivy League school with high test scores and several physical requirements. The couple defended themselves by saying that they wanted a child that would be as similar to them as possible.

So, if you're female and ready to take hormones, gain weight, have surgery, and make a few thousand dollars while helping an eggless couple, apply. Just remember that this IS a surgical procedure, so it shouldn't be taken lightly.

Adapted from "So You Wanna Donate an Egg?" with permission. Copyright © SOYOUWANNA.com

Too Old to Be Pregnant?

More and more women are turning to medical science to become mothers. Advances in reproductive technologies have made it increasingly possible for women in their 40s and 50s to give birth. Even women who are no longer fertile can use the eggs of younger donors. In 2002, the National Center for Health Statistics in the United States reported 263 births among women 50 and older, a ten-percent increase from the previous year. By comparison, the total number of babies born in the United States in 2002 was 4,021,726. This trend is raising a number of medical and ethical questions. Is there a point when a woman is too old to have a baby? We think there is.

Last week, a 66-year-old Romanian woman gave birth to a healthy baby girl. For the moment, Adriana Iliescu is the world's oldest known mother. It wasn't easy. She had to undergo nine years of fertility treatment in order to force her body to produce eggs. Then she was artificially inseminated with sperm from an anonymous donor. (In artificial insemination, a doctor injects semen into a woman's uterus.)

Ms. Iliescu, a retired university professor and the author of several children's books, is very optimistic about her future as a mother. She says that the people in her family are very long-lived, so she expects to be able to raise her daughter to adulthood without a problem.

Ms. Iliescu is not the only woman to conceive a child after the age of 60. In 2003, a 65-year-old Indian woman gave birth to a son. Schoolteacher Satyabhama Mahapatra was impregnated with an egg from her 26-year-old niece. The egg had been fertilized by Mrs. Mahapatra's husband using in-vitro fertilization. In this procedure, egg and sperm are combined in a laboratory. As a result, the couple, who had been married for 50 years, was able to have their first child.

While it is not difficult to understand the joy that these people must feel about the birth of their long-awaited offspring, one has to wonder about children raised by elderly parents. It is true that it is not unusual for men to become fathers late in life. However, until now, their children had at least one parent of the normal age for childrearing.

Adapted from "Romanian woman gives birth at 66," BBC News Online, with permission. Copyright © 2005 BBC.

Surrogate Motherhood Can Create Unusual Family Ties

NEW YORK—More and more women are offering to be surrogate mothers for childless couples. A surrogate mother is a woman who carries another woman's child. Sometimes the surrogate is artificially inseminated with the husband's sperm. Sometimes doctors implant an already fertilized egg. Some women become surrogates for money. Some do it to help friends and relatives. Here are two surrogates' stories.

Twins Born Ten Days Apart

Jody Williams is a loving mother of three. When her brother and sister-in-law were unable to become pregnant, she offered to be a surrogate mother for them. (The couple's names were not released because they wanted to remain anonymous.) The doctor fertilized her sister-in-law's eggs with her brother's sperm. Then he implanted two fertilized eggs in Williams and two in her sister-in-law. After a few weeks, tests showed that both women were pregnant.

Nine months later, the couple became the parents of fraternal twins born to different women in two different states on two different dates. Jody Williams delivered a girl on April 26. Her sister-in-law had a baby boy on May 7.

Williams and her husband, Dean, have three children of their own. "Our children accepted that this wasn't our baby," she said, "and that we would send their little cousin home to their aunt and uncle."

Williams's sister-in-law said, "We can't thank her enough. She is a great mother. She has three beautiful children that she loves and adores, and she wanted her brother and me to have that, too."

Woman Gives Birth to Grandchildren

Tina Cade gave birth to her daughter 29 years ago. Then, at 55, she gave birth to her daughter's three children. Cade's daughter, Camille Hammond, and her husband, Jason, had tried in-vitro fertilization, but the procedure was unsuccessful. Cade offered to be a surrogate for the couple.

Fertility experts said there are more and more cases of family surrogates. Couples choose a family member to be a surrogate to avoid the legal problems that can happen with a stranger. But family surrogacy has problems of its own. For example, the law in many places says that the woman who gives birth to a baby is the legal mother, even if she is a surrogate. There are also possible health problems for the surrogate — especially if she is older. Such cases can also create unusual, sometimes difficult problems for family relationships. "Someone who has carried a child for nine months may want to be more than a traditional grandmother," said Lori B. Andrews, who studies reproductive issues at the Chicago-Kent College of Law.

For her part, Camille Hammond said she hopes the birth of the children will help other couples. "We just wanted to let people know . . . there may in fact be options they haven't considered that may be a little nontraditional."

Reading Comprehension

Check Your Predictions

1. Look back at questions 1–4 in the Predict section. How accurate were your predictions?

Prediction	Not Accurate	Accurate
1a		
1b		
2a		
2b		
2c		
3		
4a		
4b		
4c		

2. If you found the answers to your questions, what were they?

Reading 1 _____

Reading 2 _____

Reading 3 _____

Check the Facts

Check (✓) the questions you can answer after reading once. Then go back and look for the answers that you are unsure of.

READING 1

_____ 1. What do Harvard, Princeton, the University of Pennsylvania, and Yale have in common?

_____ 2. Which two of these qualities did the advertisement NOT ask for?

intelligence musical ability height beauty hair color athletic ability

_____ 3. How much did the couple offer to pay for an egg?

_____ 4. Why did people criticize the couple?

_____ 5. What was their defense?

_____ 6. Why are egg donors paid more than sperm donors?

READING 2

_____ 1. How many women over 50 had babies in the United States in 2002? In 2001?

_____ 2. How old was the Romanian woman who had a child?

_____ 3. How long did she receive fertility treatments?

_____ 4. Who was the father of her child?

_____ 5. How old was the Indian woman?

_____ 6. How long had she and her husband been married?

_____ 7. Who is the genetic mother of their child?

READING 3

_____ 1. What is a surrogate mother?

_____ 2. Are all surrogate mothers the genetic mothers of the children they carry?

_____ 3. Who were the genetic parents of Jody Williams's "daughter?"

_____ 4. What do you think Jody Williams's "daughter" will call her?

_____ 5. What is Tina Cade's relationship to Camille Hammond?

_____ 6. What are the advantages of having a family member as a surrogate?

_____ 7. What are some potential problems of having a family member as a surrogate?

Vocabulary Work

Guess Meaning from Context

1. Look for these words in the readings.

Word	Reading	Meaning
candidates	1	_____
sperm	1	_____
limited	1	_____
elitist	1	_____
surgery	1	_____
donor	1	_____
trend	2	_____
ethical	2	_____
conceive	2	_____
anonymous	2 & 3	_____
fraternal	3	_____

Sometimes writers define unknown words and phrases in the reading itself. This is particularly true when they use words that are probably not familiar to the general public.

2. Find definitions for these phrases:

   artificial insemination

   _____

   in-vitro fertilization

   _____

   surrogate mother

   _____

Idioms *and* **colloquial phrases** *can be a problem for nonnative speakers. However, they can often be analyzed in the same way as vocabulary items.*

3. Can you guess the meaning of these words and phrases?

   turn to

   _____

   taken lightly

   _____

   give birth

   _____

Guess Meaning from Related Words

Another very important strategy is to relate new words to words that you already know.

1. <u>Underline</u> the common words in these compound words and phrases. Can you guess their meanings?

Word	Reading	Meaning
undergo	1	_____
increasingly	2	_____
long-lived	2	_____
long-awaited	2	_____

Often a reading contains different forms of the same word.

2. Find other forms of these words in the readings.

donate _____

elite _____

surgeon _____

semen _____

fertile _____

3. Work in pairs. Put the words from Exercise 2 in the correct columns. Compare your work with another pair when you are done.

Noun (person)	Noun (thing)	Verb	Adjective	Adverb

4. Look at the meanings of these prefixes and suffixes. Then look in the readings for the words that use them. Write the words below. Guess their meanings.

Word part	Meaning	Word	Meaning
im-	in	_____	_____
non-	not	_____	_____
-less	without	_____	_____
un-	not	_____	_____

Analyze

1. A number of different fertilization methods were used in the cases described in the readings. Which methods were used in each case?

Case	Artificial insemination	In-vitro fertilization	Third-party egg donor
Adrianna Iliescu			
Satyabhama Mahapatra			
Jody Williams			
Tina Cade			

2. Check the column that describes each woman's relationship to the baby pertaining to her story.

Case	Genetic mother	Birth mother	Caregiving mother
Adrianna Iliescu			
Satyabhama Mahapatra			
Jody Williams			
Jody's sister-in-law			
Tina Cade			
Camille Hammond			

Reading Skills

Understanding the Author's Purpose

1. The author of each article had a different purpose. Identify the purpose of each one.

   instruct   persuade   warn   describe

   Reading 1

   _____

   Reading 2

   _____

   Reading 3

   _____

2. Find language in each reading that supports your opinion.

   Reading 1

   _____

   Reading 2

   _____

   Reading 3

   _____

Discussion

1. Do you think egg donors are generous humanitarians? Why or why not?
2. Are you disturbed by any of the four cases described here? Why or why not?

PART II

This reading is more difficult than the articles in Part I. Read it for the main ideas. Do not worry if you cannot understand everything.

Read It

Read to find the answers to these questions.

1. What was wrong with the Whitakers' son?
2. Why did they decide to have another child?
3. Why did they have to go to the United States?
4. What was the difference between the Whitakers' case and the Hashmis' case?
5. Why are some people worried about selecting embryos?

 READING

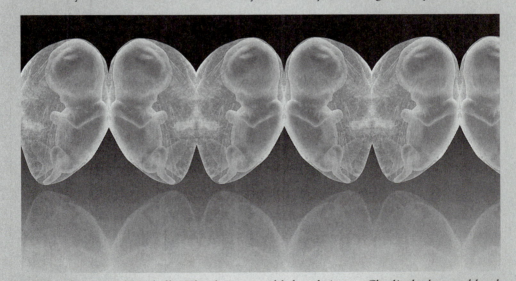

Designer Baby Transplant

A British boy with a rare blood disorder may be saved by his "designer baby" brother.

When Jayson and Michelle Whitaker were told that their son, Charlie, had a rare blood condition, they were devastated. The doctors said that Charlie's only hope for surviving Diamond Blackfan Anaemia was a stem-cell transplant. The Whitakers and their daughter, Emily, were tested, but none of them qualified as a suitable candidate to help Charlie. They were not a close enough genetic match.

(Continued on next page)

That is when the couple decided to have another child. The Whitakers, who are British, asked the government for permission to use in-vitro fertilization to create and select an embryo that would be a match for Charlie. When permission was denied, the Whitakers went to the United States, where such procedures are not illegal.

Charlie's newest sibling, Jamie, was born after being selected from a number of embryos as a perfect genetic match. Blood was collected from his umbilical cord to be used for Charlie's transplant. The Whitakers have to wait until Jamie is six months old to make sure that he does not have the same blood disease as Charlie before the stem-cell transplant can be done.

Controversy

According to the Whitakers, they just did what they had to do to save their child. However, others do not agree. There has been considerable argument in the United Kingdom about the selecting of embryos. Critics worry that such selection could lead to babies being created to provide spare parts. But the boys' father, Jayson Whitaker, said there was no selection on the basis of color of eyes or hair or sex: "All we did was change the odds from a one-in-four chance of a match (from a baby conceived naturally) to a 98 percent chance."

Sometimes, the line between the permissible and the impermissible is difficult to see. Last year, the British government gave another couple, Shahana and Raj Hashmi, permission to test their unborn child to make sure his/her tissue would be a suitable match for their 4-year-old son, Zain, who suffers from a rare blood disorder. Neither the couple nor their four other children were bone-marrow matches for Zain, who was expected to die without a transplant. In the Hashmis' case, the boy's illness was hereditary. Screening the new baby would be necessary anyway to ensure the new child did not have the disease. The doctors simply performed one more test to see if the embryo was a match for Zain. But Charlie Whitaker's condition is not usually inherited, so there was no reason to test the embryo for the disease.

Dr. Lana Rechitsky, a doctor at the Chicago institute that treated the Whitakers, doesn't understand why the procedure is so controversial. She said, "We are not creating anything new. We are just trying to choose between the embryos to find the one that is normal and can save the life of its sibling." A spokeswoman from Comment on Reproductive Ethics (CORE) disagrees: "CORE believes that the designing of a child as a tissue donor for a sick sibling is undesirable, unnecessary, and that the current decision-making process is profoundly undemocratic."

Vocabulary Work

Guess Meaning from Context

1. Do you need to understand all of these words to answer the prereading questions?

devastated	embryo	sibling	genetic	umbilical cord
considerable	spare parts	permissible	impermissible	disorder
spokeswoman	inherited	controversial	profoundly	undemocratic

2. Can you guess the meanings of the words important to understanding the reading? What clues did you use? Write the words from Exercise 1 under the corresponding clues you used to understand their meanings.

It looks like a word I know.

_____

I guessed from an example.

_____

I used my knowledge of the world.

_____

I understood the prefix or suffix.

_____

There is a definition or a synonym in the reading.

_____

Reading Skills

Identifying Main Ideas and Evaluating Types of Supporting Details

Writers use different types of supporting details to expand on their main ideas.

Types of Supporting Details

Description: Mali is a wild and beautiful place with stark mountains rising against a bright blue sky.

Example: Children need structure. In my sister's house, there are no set bedtimes or mealtimes and, as a result, her children have a terrible time obeying rules in school.

Statistics: Most people in our town would like to build a new school. In a recent survey, 66 percent of the population said that they would be willing to pay higher taxes in order to have a modern school.

Expert: Our local economy is doing much better than the national average. Dr. Tania Butler, economics professor at Gainesboro University, says that this is because of our low taxes and the high number of skilled workers in the local population.

Look back at the reading. First, identify the main ideas. Then decide on the type of supporting details the writer uses to expand on each one. Circle examples to share.

Idea Exchange

Think about Your Ideas

Look at the list of procedures below. What is your opinion of each of them?

   a.   I would undergo this procedure.

   b.   I would not undergo this procedure under any circumstances.

   c.   I would not let my spouse undergo this procedure under any circumstances.

   d.   I would undergo this procedure for a close friend or family member.

   e.   I would undergo this procedure for a stranger.

   f.   This procedure should not be allowed.

   g.   This procedure should only be allowed in very special circumstances.

   h.   This procedure should be allowed if the parents want it.

   i.   I prefer not to respond.

1.   Hormone treatments to increase a woman's number of eggs. _____
2.   In-vitro fertilization with the sperm and egg of the parents. _____
3.   In-vitro fertilization with egg or sperm from a donor. _____
4.   Implantation of a fertilized egg in the mother. _____
5.   Implantation of a fertilized egg in a surrogate. _____
6.   Artificial insemination with sperm from a donor. _____
7.   Selection of an embryo to make sure that it does not have a serious hereditary disease. _____
8.   Selection of an embryo to find a donor for a sick sibling. _____
9.   Selection of an embryo for gender. _____
10. Selection of an embryo for physical characteristics. _____

Talk about Your Ideas

1.   Is there any difference between the procedures that you would be willing to undergo and the ones that you think other people should be allowed to have? Why or why not?

2.   Clearly there is a lot of controversy and confusion about the ethics of these medical procedures. Who should make the policies regarding their legality? Should it be doctors? the government? religious leaders? Give reasons for your opinions.

For CNN video activities about surrogacy, turn to page 193.

CHAPTER 4

Gambling:
Wanna' bet?

a.

b.

e.

c.

d.

PREVIEW

1. Match the words and the pictures. Which ones are forms of gambling?

   poker _____   roulette _____   slot machine _____   Bingo _____   lottery _____

2. Are these games legal in your country? If so, do many people play?

3. Are there any other popular gambling games in your country?

PART I

Predict

A. Skim the readings and make predictions.

1. Look at the title and the subtitles of each reading.
   a. The topic of Reading 1 is probably _____.
   b. The topic of Reading 2 is probably _____.

2. Look at the format of each reading and ⟨circle⟩ the format type that fits.
   a. Reading 1 probably comes from a
      - newspaper
      - textbook
      - journal
   b. Reading 2 probably comes from a
      - newspaper
      - textbook
      - journal

3. Skim each reading for new vocabulary or new sentence structures. Predict and ⟨circle⟩ the level of difficulty.
   a. Reading 1 will probably be easy / a little difficult / very difficult.
   b. Reading 2 will probably be easy / a little difficult / very difficult.

B. Write a question that you think each reading will answer.

Reading 1

_____

Reading 2

_____

Read It

Read the articles and look for the answers to your questions.

 **READING 1**

My Job? I'm a Gambler.

1 **Greg Lawrence is an engineer, but he would rather play poker than build roads.**

2   When people ask about my work, I just say, "I play poker." At first, I was
3 embarrassed to talk about my "job." Then I saw that most people were really interested.
4 They wanted to know all about it. You probably do, too. So, here is the story.

5   I make about $40 an hour. I only play poker about 30 hours a week, so I have a lot
6 of time for other activities. For example, I love tennis. I spend a lot of time on the tennis
7 court. I do not think about gambling when I am playing tennis. Playing poker is my job.
8 Playing tennis is fun.

9 **My Poker Face**

10   I play poker on the Internet. In some ways, this is very different from playing in a
11 casino. First, online poker is a lot faster because no one talks during the game. Some
12 people do not like online poker for this reason. They want to hear the other players talk.
13 They also want to be able to watch the other players. These players know a lot about body
14 language. They use this knowledge to help them. In poker, you have to be able to lie or
15 *bluff.* That means that in casino poker, players need to have a *poker face.* When you have a
16 poker face, no one knows if your cards are good or bad. I am not good at this, so I don't
17 like playing in a casino.

18   Once, when I went to a casino, I got a hand of really good cards. I could not stop
19 smiling, so I could not bluff. Online, I can bluff with a perfect poker face. No one knows
20 if I am lying.

21 **My Strategy**

22   There is no secret about the way I play. The most common mistake that beginners
23 make is not stopping early enough. When your cards are bad, you have to stop.

24   My biggest wins have been about the same as my biggest losses. I once lost $5,000 in
25 one day, but I have also won the same amount in one day. My first big loss came when I
26 had just begun playing online. I started with only $300 and in three months I had
27 $4,000. I became overconfident. I thought I knew it all. Then I lost $1,500 in one day.
28 That destroyed my confidence. I thought I would never play again. After a while, I read
29 some books on poker strategies. Then I started playing again.

30   I do not plan to make this my career forever. I would like to get married and have
31 children one day. I do not want to have to tell my children that I am a professional
32 gambler. It is not illegal, but it does not seem like a serious job. For me, playing poker is
33 just a temporary job. I am not sure how long I will continue, but it has been fun.

READING 2

Taking a Gamble

1 **Gambling is big business and some people say that's a problem.**

Experts say that more North Americans are gambling now than in the past. Although gambling is against the law in most of the United States, it is now legal in many places. Five states have gambling casinos, 36 have lotteries, and at least 18 have gambling on
5 Indian reservations.[1] Each year, Americans bet $300 billion legally and about $40 billion illegally. However, since bettors win some of that money back, the gambling industry makes (and gamblers lose) about $35 billion.

For some people, gambling is a casual hobby or just fun. However, for others, it is a problem. The National Gambling Impact Study Commission says that there are about
10 three million *problem gamblers* in the United States. Another two million are *compulsive gamblers. Problem gamblers* are people who gamble more money than they can afford to spend. *Compulsive gambling* is even more serious. It is a disease. Edward Looney, from the Council on Compulsive Gambling of New Jersey says, "The compulsive gambler cannot stop".

Many people with gambling problems join Gamblers Anonymous (GA). GA is a
15 group of people who share their experiences with gambling in order to help themselves and others. Do you have a gambling problem? Answer these questions and find out. Most compulsive gamblers will answer *yes* to at least seven of these questions:

    1. Did you ever miss work or school due to gambling?
    2. Has gambling ever made your home life unhappy?
20   3. Have you ever felt bad after gambling?
    4. Have you ever gambled to pay bills?
    5. After you lose, do you want to return quickly to win back your money?
    6. After winning, do you want to return and win more?
    7. Do you often gamble until you have no money?
25   8. Do you borrow money to gamble?
    9. Do you sell things to get money for gambling?
    10. Do you want to gamble when you are worried?
    11. Does gambling cause you to have trouble sleeping?
    12. Do you want to gamble when you feel angry or disappointed?
30   13. Do you celebrate good fortune by gambling?

Gamblers Anonymous is free, but members donate small amounts for materials. Most U.S. cities have regular meetings and the addresses can be found at the Web site: www.gamblersanonymous.org.

[1]An Indian reservation is land that belongs to an Indian or Native American tribe. The U.S. government allows gambling on Indian land even in states where gambling is illegal.

Reading Comprehension

Check Your Predictions

1. Look back at questions 1 and 2 in the Predict section. How accurate were your predictions?

Prediction	Not Accurate	Accurate
1a		
1b		
2a		
2b		
3a		
3b		

2. If you found the answers to your questions, what were they?

Reading 1 _____

Reading 2 _____

Check the Facts

Check (✓) the questions you can answer after reading the first article once. Then go back and look for the answers you are unsure of.

READING 1

_____ 1. Is Greg Lawrence embarrassed about his "job" now? Why or why not?

_____ 2. How much money does he make?

_____ 3. How many hours does he work in a week?

_____ 4. What does he do in his free time?

_____ 5. How is online poker different from casino poker?

_____ 6. Why does Greg prefer online poker?

_____ 7. What is Greg's advice to new players?

_____ 8. What is the most he has lost in one day? won in one day?

_____ 9. Why did he almost quit playing when he first started?

_____ 10. Does he plan to play poker to earn an income for his whole life? Why or why not?

READING 2

Read to find the answer to these questions.

1. What is …
    a. a person who gambles for fun? _____
    b. a problem gambler? _____
    c. a compulsive gambler? _____
2. What are some signs that a person has a gambling problem?

Analyze

Read between the lines

1. Why do you think Greg used to be embarrassed about his job?
2. Why does Greg say, "I do not think about gambling when I am playing tennis. Playing poker is my job. Playing tennis is fun."
3. Why is it important to be able to have a poker face when playing casino poker?

Vocabulary Work

Guess Meaning from Related Words

There are a number of words in the readings that pertain to gambling and poker playing. Find other forms of these words from the readings.

1. bet   _____
2. legal   _____ _____
3. gamble   _____

Guess Meaning from Context

1. Work with a partner. Look back at Reading 1 and guess the meaning of each word.

Word	Line	Guess	Match
a. bluff	_____	_____	_____
b. casino	_____	_____	_____
c. hand	_____	_____	_____
d. poker face	_____	_____	_____

2. Turn to page 49 and match the correct meaning with each word.
3. Look at the words you guessed correctly. Look back at the reading. What clues did you use?

Analyzing Words and Phrases

A. You can sometimes guess the meaning of new words by looking at their context. Look at these examples:

> I played poker, but I didn't **win.**
>
> I've had big **wins.**
>
> Everyone wants to be a **winner.**

1. Put the words in bold in the chart below.

2. Look back at the readings and complete the chart with the correct forms of the words you find in the readings.

Verb	Noun (person)	Noun (thing)
win		
bet		
gamble		

3. Find words in the readings that are related to these words:

profession _____

short-term _____

confidence _____

know _____

B. Look at these phrases. Can you guess their meanings?

Phrases	Line	Meaning
body language		
against the law		

Discussion

1. What do you think about Greg's job?

2. Do you think Greg will stop playing poker and get a more traditional job? Why or why not?

3. Would you gamble instead of working if you could?

> Answers to Exercise 1 in Guess Meaning from Context on page 48.
> **a.** to make people think your hand (the total of the cards in your hand) is better than it really is
> **b.** a place where people gamble
> **c.** the cards that you are holding
> **d.** not smiling or frowning

PART II

This reading is more difficult than the articles in Part I. Read it for the main ideas. Do not worry if you cannot understand everything.

Read It

Read to find the answers to these questions.

1. Why does the author say that gambling doesn't "make sense"?
2. What was the author's system for winning at roulette?
3. What mistake do new gamblers make?
4. Why does the author think that people gamble?
5. How is gambling like sex?

 READING

The Allure of Gambling
by David Spanier

Suppose a friend offered you a deal. "Hey, let's toss a coin for a dollar, heads or tails." "Ok," you might say, but then your friend adds, "There's just one little thing I want to explain before we start. When I win, you lose your dollar. When you win, I'll pay you 99 cents."

It's not all that different, is it, one penny on the toss? But you would be crazy to take on such a proposition, wouldn't you? A dollar to 99 cents. Why do it? It makes no sense.

But that is exactly what all of us do when we gamble, when we cross the threshold between workaday life and the fantasy world of a casino. In fact, if the house gets only one percent of an edge, or advantage, gamblers consider it a good bet.

Most people do not really understand how odds work. Before my first visit to Las Vegas, I thought I had worked out a pretty good system for roulette. My plan was to wait for a series of reds or blacks—at least six in a row. When that happened, I would start betting on the other color, doubling up after each losing bet until I won. For instance, after six reds in a row, I would start betting black: $1, then $2, $4, $8, $16, $32, $64, $128. I figured that I couldn't lose unless the same color came up 15 times in a row. This seemed highly unlikely.

I watched for a while and then I saw my chance—six blacks in a row. I bet red and lost. I bet red again. The wheel stopped on black for the eighth time . . . the ninth . . . the tenth . . . the eleventh . . . the twelfth . . . the thirteenth . . . . Suddenly I realized my "perfect" system was flawed. I had lost $255 and had to bet $255 more on the next spin. I quit.

Now I know that this is a mistake that almost all beginning gamblers make. They confuse the short-term outcome with the long-term probability. On every individual spin, the probability of red or black is the same—fifty-fifty. Over thousands of spins, reds and blacks will eventually even out. But within that series, there will be many short-term inequalities. Fourteen reds in a row is not unusual.

Casino gambling is risk taking in its purest form. The participants willingly agree to play although they know that the odds are not in their favor. The question is why do people still do it?

You might think that they gamble for money—they don't. Not that money isn't important. It is. You can't gamble without money—it's just not fun. You also can't drive a car without gasoline—the car won't move. But the pleasure of driving is not about gas. It's about speed and movement. And so the pleasure of gambling is about taking a risk—the rush of adrenaline that you get between the time you place your bet and when you know if you have won or lost.

This is what casinos offer gamblers—short-term thrills. Casino gamblers look down on lotteries because the chance of winning is too small. However, slot machines, dice, blackjack, and roulette can provide an immediate return. At a fast-moving game of roulette, there may be more than 60 spins in an hour, a slot machine offers perhaps five or six chances a minute. In fact, with a slot machine, the thrill of the action is almost continuous—as long as the money lasts.

The gambling games offered by casinos act like a drug. It's part physical, part psychological, highs and lows, over and over, in rapid succession. For gamblers, living on the edge is exciting. Some psychologists have suggested a parallel between gambling and sexual excitement—build up, climax, release of tension, all repeated over and over. There is no need to press the analogy too far to make the point that gambling carries a strong emotional charge.

Reprinted from "The Joy of Gambling," The Wilson Quarterly, Vol 19, with permission. Copyright © 1995 David Spanier

Vocabulary Work

Guess Meaning from Context

1. Do you need to understand all of these words to answer the prereading questions? Cross out (~~word~~) the words and phrases that you can ignore and still answer the questions. <u>Underline</u> the words you know. (Circle) the words you need to guess.

allure	odds	rush of
toss	roulette	adrenaline
heads or tails	flawed	look down on
a proposition	outcome	slot machines
cross the threshold	short-term	dice
workaday	inequalities	blackjack
the house	in their favor	living on the edge
an edge		

2. Try to use the following kinds of clues to help you understand the words. Remember, it is often necessary to put several clues together in order to make a good guess.

> It looks like a word I know.
>
> I understood the prefix or suffix.
>
> I used my knowledge of gambling.
>
> I used logic.
>
> I used general world knowledge.
>
> The writer gave a synonym, definition, or explanation.
>
> The writer gave an example.
>
> The word occurs in a list and I know some of the words in the list.

Reading Skills

Identifying the Author's Opinion

1. Does the author state his opinion about gambling openly? If not, does he give you some clues?

2. How did the author used to feel about gambling? Has his opinion changed? Support your opinion with information from the reading.

3. How does the author feel about gambling now? Give a reason for your answer.

Idea Exchange

Think about Your Ideas

1. Do you ever play any of these games for money? If so, how often?

Do you ever . . .	Never	Once or twice a year	A few times a year	Once or twice a month	Once or twice a week
play bingo?					
buy lottery tickets?					
bet on races?					
play slot machines or video poker?					
play poker?					
play casino games?					

2. How much money does gambling cost you a year?

   approximate amount I spend $ _____

   approximate amount I win   − $ _____
   _____

   gambling costs me about $ _____ a year

3. How do you feel when you are gambling? Circle the adjectives that describe your emotions.

depressed	out of control
independent	sophisticated
rich	happy
excited	poor
nervous	strong
scared	in control
free	weak

4. How do you feel when you lose?

Talk about Your Ideas

1. Is gambling a social problem? Can you be addicted to gambling? Why or why not?

2. Should the government regulate gambling? Why or why not?

3. Do you gamble? If so, why? If not, why not?

For CNN video activities about gambling, turn to page 194.

CHAPTER 5

THE DISABLED: HANDICAPPED? NOT US!

d.

c.

a.

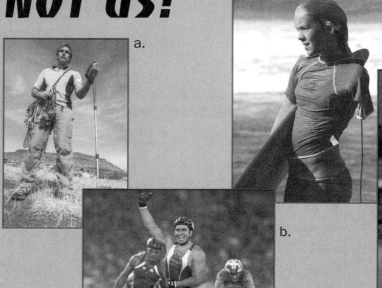

e.

b.

PREVIEW

Discuss these questions with your classmates.

1. Do you know any of these people? Who are they?
2. What do you think when you see people like the people pictured above?

(Names and achievements on next page)

PART I

Predict

A. Skim the two readings and make predictions.

1. Which reading . . .
   a. comes from a newspaper?
   b. was probably written by a group that helps the handicapped?
   c. talks about a specific type of handicap?
   d. was meant to inform the public?

2. Predict difficulty of each reading.
   a. Reading 1

   very easy   pretty easy   difficult   very difficult

   b. Reading 2

   very easy   pretty easy   difficult   very difficult

B. Write a question that you think each reading will answer.

Reading 1

_____

Reading 2

_____

Read It

Read the articles and look for the answers to your questions.

 READING 1

Common Myths and Stereotypes about Disabilities

Myth: A person with a disability is sick or has something wrong with them.

Fact: Disability is a natural part of the human experience, and it is not the same as being sick. Individuals with disabilities have varying degrees of need and are sometimes sick, just as nondisabled are sometimes sick. Mistaking a disability for sickness not only fails to respond to a person's needs, it perpetuates a negative stereotype and an assumption that the disabled person can and should be cured.

Myth: People with disabilities have a poor quality of life.

Fact: This is one of the most common and damaging stereotypes because it discourages social interactions and the development of mature relationships with disabled people. People with disabilities have social needs just like those who are nondisabled. They work for a high degree of quality of life just as we do. Sometimes society itself makes the life of disabled people more difficult. For example, individuals in wheelchairs may not be able to enter restaurants, theaters, buses, etc., if ramps and handrails are not provided.

Myth: People with disabilities are inspirational, brave, and courageous for living successfully with their disability.

Fact: A person with a disability is simply carrying out normal activities of living when they drive to work, go shopping, pay their bills, or compete in athletic events. Some of the disabled *are* heroic, just as some nondisabled people are. However, simply living with a disability is not heroic.

Myth: People with disabilities always need expensive and high-tech devices or services.

Fact: Simple inexpensive devices are often the most important devices in helping people with a disability live independently. Such devices can be as affordable as an eating utensil or Velcro strap.

Myth: People with severe disabilities need to live in hospitals or under constant supervision so that they do not hurt themselves.

Fact: Even those with the most severe disabilities can often live in their own home with adequate community services.

Reprinted from www.acils.com with permission. Copyright © Access Center for Independent Living

The Deaf Say, "Don't Try to Cure Us—Accept Us!"

In the future, we may be calling the disabled, the "differenced." Because that's what some disabled groups say they are. They see their handicap or disability as another characteristic such as being left-handed. Many people identify so strongly with their disability that they cannot imagine being themselves without it. One of the most vocal groups are the Deaf. (Many prefer to use an uppercase "D," to emphasize their group identity like "the Irish" or "the French.")

Unlike the blind, who can communicate verbally, the Deaf have traditionally been more isolated from society. This isolation has helped them create an extremely strong and cohesive community. Years ago, it was common for deaf children to be taught to lip-read so that they could be a part of the dominant hearing culture. Today, although many learn to lip-read as a convenience, American Sign Language (ASL) is the first language of most deaf people. No one who has seen deaf people animatedly talking to each other can doubt that ASL is as an effective means of communication as any other language.

In the age of "Sign Language Barbie" dolls, it may be difficult to believe society's prejudice against deaf people and their unique form of communication. For example, in biblical times, the Deaf were not allowed to own property. As recently as the last century, innovators like Alexander Graham Bell campaigned against sign language. He even believed that deaf people should not intermarry because they would be likely to have deaf children. These kinds of attitudes only strengthened the cohesion of the deaf community and helped them to create a distinct culture.

However, today some deaf people feel that this distinct culture may be in danger. Technological advances are changing the way deaf people communicate and the way they meet. For example, in the past, deaf people socialized in big groups at clubs created for the deaf population. Today, such clubs are disappearing because deaf people can stay home and watch closed-captioned televisions with their hearing friends and send text messages to each other via the Internet.

In recent years, medical science has learned how to perform an operation that enables people with very limited hearing to greatly improve their hearing. This controversial medical procedure is known as a cochlear implant. Opinions about the implants have split the deaf world. Some believe that the operation is unnecessary and that it is a rejection of deaf culture. Indeed, those who have the operation are often shunned by their former deaf friends. As one deaf activist put it, "In the United States it's easier to be white than black, but does that mean black people would welcome an operation to become white?"

Some fear that these changes in medical science could signal the gradual disappearance of deaf culture. Others point to the deaf community's rich history and language as proof that deaf culture cannot be destroyed by technology alone.

Reading Comprehension

Check Your Predictions

1. Look back at questions 1 and 2 in the Predict section. How accurate were your predictions?

Prediction	Not Accurate	Accurate
1a		
1b		
1c		
1d		
2a		
2b		

2. If you found the answers to your questions, what were they?

Reading 1: _____

Reading 2: _____

Check the Facts

READING 1

Write T for *true*, F for *false*, or NS for *not sure.*

_____ 1. A disability is a sickness.

_____ 2. The lives of disabled people are similar to the lives of nondisabled people.

_____ 3. We should admire disabled people who live independently.

_____ 4. Some tools and devices for the disabled are very inexpensive.

_____ 5. Most disabled people are not given the choice to live on their own.

READING 2

Check (✓) the questions you can answer after reading once. Then go back and look for the answers that you are unsure of.

_____ 1. How is being deaf different from being blind?

_____ 2. What is the purpose of lip-reading? ASL?

_____ 3. How were the Deaf discriminated against in the past?

_____ 4. What is threatening deaf culture today?

_____ 5. What is a cochlear implant?

_____ 6. Why are some people against this procedure?

_____ 7. What does one deaf person compare cochlear implants to?

Analyze

1. Which of the myths in Reading 1 might apply to how people viewed the Deaf in the past?

2. Are there any myths or stories that people may still believe today?

Vocabulary Work

Guess Meaning from Context

1. Look for the words in the table in the readings. Decide if they are necessary to understanding the authors' main ideas. Use these types of clues to guess the meaning of the important ones:

   a. knowledge of social attitudes

   b. knowledge of the Deaf

   c. logic

   d. examples in the reading

   e. definitions or synonyms in the reading

Word	Reading	Type of clue	Meaning
assumption	1	_____	_____
carry out	1	_____	_____
devices	1	_____	_____
utensil	1	_____	_____
Velcro	1	_____	_____
severe	1	_____	_____
constant	1	_____	_____
adequate	1	_____	_____
animatedly	2	_____	_____
unique	2	_____	_____
innovators	2	_____	_____
campaigned	2	_____	_____
distinct	2	_____	_____
advances	2	_____	_____
closed-captioned	2	_____	_____
shunned	2	_____	_____

2. Discuss what these items of contemporary culture signify.

    "Sign Language Barbie" dolls

    closed-captioned

Guess Meaning from Related Words

1. Underline the common words in these compound words and phrases. Guess the meaning.

Word or Phrase	Reading	Meaning
wheelchair	1	_____
sign language	2	_____
lip-read	2	_____

2. Find other forms of these words in the readings.

READING 1

able	_____
hero	_____
damage	_____
afford	_____
social	_____

READING 2

voice	_____
convenient	_____
reject	_____
cohere	_____
bible	_____
active	_____
dominate	_____
social	_____

3. Work in pairs. Put the words from Exercise 2 in the correct columns on page 61. Compare your work with another pair when you are done.

Noun (person)	Noun (thing)	Verb	Adjective	Adverb

4. Look at the meanings of these prefixes. Then look for the words that use them and guess their meanings.

Prefix	Meaning	Word(s) from readings	Possible meaning
inter-	between	_____	_____
non-	not	_____	_____

Reading Skills

Identifying Time Markers

It is important to notice words and phrases that tell you when something happened. This is particularly true in articles such as Reading 2 which moves between the past, present, and future.

Look at the reading and identify the time markers.

(*Hint:* There are at least eight.)

Discussion

1. Do you believe that the Deaf have a distinct culture? Why or why not?
2. Do you agree with the Deaf activist's analogy comparing Deaf people to blacks in the United States? Why or why not?

PART II

This reading is more difficult than the articles in Part I. Read it for the main ideas. Do not worry if you cannot understand everything.

Read It

Read to find the answers to these questions.

1. What are some of Kyle Maynard's accomplishments?
2. What did the writer mean by his "passionate normality"?
3. When did Kyle's handicap develop?
4. How did his parents treat him?
5. Why did Kyle quit football?
6. Was he successful at wrestling in the beginning?
7. What did he and his coach do?
8. What is one of Kyle's favorite sayings?
9. What else is he doing now?
10. What blessing does Kyle say that he has been given?

 READING

Kyle Maynard: Diminutive Giant

Most people seeing a picture of Kyle Maynard for the first time feel shock and then a stab of sorrow or sympathy for the young man with the severely shortened limbs. Then, on hearing his accomplishments, that same person might be filled with admiration for his perseverance. This list includes being an honor role student, one of the top high school wrestlers in Georgia, a recipient of ESPN's ESPY Award for best athlete with a disability, and a recipient of the Courage Award from the World Sports Humanitarian Hall of Fame.

However, for me, meeting Kyle in person invoked none of those emotions. I was simply overwhelmed by his "passionate normality." He clearly didn't want to be admired. He wanted to be thought of as a normal guy with an interesting difference. "I really feel like I'm average," Maynard says, smiling as he hops into his wheelchair.

Maynard was born on March 24, 1986, with a congenital defect that robbed him of arms above the elbows and his legs above the knees. His parents very soon realized that Kyle was handicapped only in the physical sense. His mental focus and drive shocked them. Watching other toddlers hold crayons in their fingers, Kyle quickly taught himself to hold objects between his two highly sensitive bicep muscles.

Kyle says that his parents are responsible for his great attitude and belief in himself. When Kyle was an infant, his father stressed self-reliance, often telling his more sympathetic wife, "If he does not figure out how to eat on his own, he's going to starve." Soon, Kyle was feeding himself using his bicep muscles. It's the same technique he uses today to grab french fries, open medicine packages, and use his tiny cell phone. This technique also enables him to have beautiful handwriting, and type 50 words per minute.

Early on, Kyle developed a passion for sports and competition. Then, when he was thirteen, he joined his school football team. Despite his determination, the game was tough on Kyle. Both of his feet were broken by opponents. "I always told Kyle, 'Don't assume you can't do something,' but even so, football was hard on him," his father told a reporter from *USA Today*. "In the end, wrestling was perfect because his opponents couldn't run from him."

However, wrestling wasn't easy in the beginning. After losing his first 35 high school matches in a row, Kyle was struggling physically and emotionally. "I was getting worried," he says. "Because losing in combat like that is very tough on the ego."

But Kyle and his coach developed fearsome moves with names like "jawbreaker" and the "buzz saw" that take advantage of Kyle's low center of gravity and great strength. These moves turned the tide, and Kyle started winning.

As impressive as his academic and sport accomplishments are, it is Kyle's attitude towards life that makes him a truly unique person. Kyle does not think in terms of limitations, but only in terms of accomplishments. A problem that the world sees as a handicap, Kyle uses as a gift. One of Kyle's favorite sayings is, "It's not what I *can* do; it's what I *will* do."

Kyle Maynard is now living his other dream—traveling across the country as a motivational speaker. He says, "The people that remain positive in tougher situations than I'll ever face, that's who I draw inspiration from." In the end, what makes him different isn't his body; it's his heart.

Asked if he ever thinks, "Why me?" he replies, "Not really. I think I've been given a tremendous blessing—being able to try to help people—and I think that's what I'm going to try to do throughout the rest of my life." Kyle Maynard may only stand three feet tall, but he is truly a giant among men.

Adapted from "Wrestler's world is never limited by his disability," USA Today, November 17, 2004 with permission.

Vocabulary Work

Guess Meaning from Context

1. Do you need to understand all of these words to answer the prereading questions? Cross out (~~word~~) the words and phrases that you can ignore from the article. <u>Underline</u> the words you know. Circle the words you need to guess.

diminutive	giant	shock	stab	sympathy
passionate	normality	admiration	congenital	defect
giant	self-reliance	sympathetic	starve	mental focus
struggling	tough	opponents	matches	in a row
combat	fearsome	moves	turned the tide	limitations
motivational	determination	blessing	perseverance	
recipient	drive	bicep muscles	center of gravity	

2. Try to use the following kinds of clues to help you understand the words. Remember that it is often necessary to put several clues together in order to make a good guess. List the words under the clue or clues you used to understand each one.

It looks like a word I know and/or I understood its prefix or suffix.

_____

I used my knowledge of wrestling and other sports.

_____

I used my knowledge of human nature.

_____

I used logic.

_____

The writer gave a definition or explanation.

_____

The writer gave an example.

_____

Reading Skills

Understanding Introductory or Fronted Phrases

In order to make their writing more interesting, writers often move adverb phrases to the beginning of a sentence. (In fact, the previous sentence uses this technique.) The normal word order would be:

> Writers often move phrases to the beginning of a sentence in order to make their writing more interesting.

Writers may also omit some words and change verb forms. It may look confusing, but you simply have to remember that the subject of the phrase is always the same as the subject of the sentence.

> Pam leaned out the window and called to the boys in the street.

> Leaning out of the window, Pam called to the boys in the street.

> The police questioned Brad about his involvement in the robbery, but he denied knowing anything about it.

> Questioned about his involvement in the robbery, Brad denied knowing anything about it.

Rewrite these sentences in normal word order. Make any other changes that are necessary.

1. Watching other toddlers hold crayons in their fingers, Kyle quickly taught himself to hold objects between his two highly sensitive bicep muscles.

   _____

   _____

2. Despite his determination, the game was tough on Kyle.

   _____

   _____

3. A problem that the world sees as a handicap, Kyle uses as a gift.

   _____

   _____

4. Asked if he ever thinks, "Why me?" he replies, "Not really."

   _____

   _____

Idea Exchange

Think about Your Ideas

1. Think about any disabled people that you know or know about. What kind of disabilities do they have? Some examples of handicaps include the following:

   blindness

   deafness

   mental handicap

   physical handicap

   learning disability

   mental illness

2. How disabled is each person on this scale?

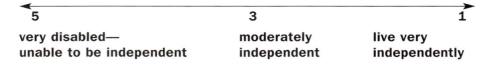

5	3	1
very disabled— **unable to be independent**	**moderately** **independent**	**live very** **independently**

3. Compare their lives to yours.

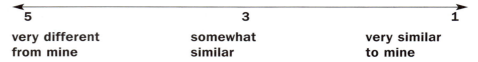

5	3	1
very different **from mine**	**somewhat** **similar**	**very similar** **to mine**

4. Does each person receive any kind of services from the community? If so, what kinds? How often?

Talking about Your Ideas

Discuss these questions with your class.

1. What kinds, if any, of accommodations should society make for handicapped people?
2. How might accommodations hurt handicapped people?
3. Do people who consider themselves "normal" have unjustified prejudices about handicapped people? How do you know?

For CNN video activities about a deaf football team, turn to page 195.

CHAPTER 6

MARRIAGE: WHY MARRY JUST ONE?

PREVIEW

Read the following quotations. Choose the one that you most agree with and the one that you least agree with.

"A successful marriage requires falling in love many times, always with the same person."

Mignon McLaughlin, American Author-Editor

"I've been married three times—and each time I married the right person."

Margaret Mead, American Anthropologist

"Rituals are important. Nowadays it's hip not to be married. I'm not interested in being hip."

John Lennon, British Rock Musician

"Bigamy is having one husband too many. Monogamy is the same."

Erica Jong, American Author

> "Two souls and one thought, two hearts and one pulse."
>
> Van Halen, American Rock Musician
>
> "Keep your eyes wide open before marriage, and half-shut afterwards."
>
> Benjamin Franklin, American Statesman and Philosopher

PART I

Predict

A. Look at the titles of the readings and make predictions. How would you classify each reading?

   a. Reading 1

      a human interest story   a scientific report   a news article   an editorial

   b. Reading 2

      a human interest story   a scientific report   a news article   an editorial

B. Skim the readings and answer the questions by circling or writing your prediction.

1. Which reading contains . . .

   a. statistics?   Reading 1   Reading 2   Both

   b. quotes from researchers?   Reading 1   Reading 2   Both

   c. quotes from ordinary people?   Reading 1   Reading 2   Both

2. Who is Thomas Green? _____

3. Predict the difficulty of each reading.

   a. Reading 1: very easy   pretty easy   difficult   very difficult

   b. Reading 2: very easy   pretty easy   difficult   very difficult

C. Write a question that you think each reading will answer.

Reading 1

_____

Reading 2

_____

Read It

Read the definition and the two articles and look for the answers to your questions.

> **Serial monogamy** is defined as a common sexual relationship pattern in contemporary Western cultures. A person may be said to be practicing serial monogamy if that person only has one sexual partner at any one time, but has had more than one sexual partner in their lifetime. Partners can be married or unmarried, but they have never more than one at a time.
>
> —from *Wikipedia,* an Internet encyclopedia
> (www.wikipedia.com)

 READING 1

Will You Still Love Me Tomorrow?
Serial monogamists say, "Maybe"

All the statistics say that Americans are voting *no* on marriage. Only 56 percent of all adults in the United States are married, compared with 75 percent 30 years ago. The proportion of traditional American households—married couple with children—has dropped to 26 percent, from 45 percent in the early 1970s. In addition, a 1999 Rutgers University study reported that only 38 percent of Americans who are on their first marriages describe themselves as happy in that state.

It's not that men and woman aren't interested in each other anymore. It's simply that more and more couples are choosing to live together rather than marry. Cohabitation used to be what people did before they got married. "Now", says Pamela Smock, a sociologist at the University of Michigan, "many couples are choosing never to marry, and, increasingly, cohabitation is seen as a substitute for marriage rather than a prelude to it." Surveys show that about 55 percent of couples who live together eventually get married. Another 40 percent end their relationship within five years.

This pattern is redefining families. Robin Baker, a British researcher on human sexual behavior, agrees. He sees a pattern of shorter relationships and greater mobility from partner to partner. He believes that technology will play a greater role in relationships. According to Baker, techniques such as in-vitro fertilization will make "coupling" unnecessary. (In-vitro is Latin for "in glass;" this is a procedure in which an egg and a sperm are combined in a test tube.) In the future, he thinks single-parent families will be normal. Is he distressed about this possibility? On the contrary, he's enthusiastic. According to him, "Single parenthood will become the best system for raising children in the 21st century."

Thirty years ago, anthropologist Margaret Mead predicted that serial marriage would become the pattern of the future. She got the "serial" part right, but the "marriage" part seems to be on its way out.

By Marilyn Gardner. Reproduced with permission from the Christian Science Monitor, March 2000 (www.csmonitor.com)
© The Christian Science Monitor. All Rights Reserved.

Polygamist Goes to Jail; Judge Ignores Pleas of His Wives and Children

Salt Lake City—A polygamist has been sentenced to five years in prison. Utah Judge Guy Burningham sentenced Thomas Green to serve five concurrent terms for four counts of bigamy and one of failing to pay child support. Green, who has argued that his Mormon background permits polygamy, could have received up to 25 years.

The husband of five and father of twenty-five lives with his family in a remote desert compound near the Utah-Nevada border. He has told interviewers that polygamy is a 150-year-old tradition of Mormon culture, and he will not give it up even if it means going to prison.

The Mormon Church itself gave up polygamy in the 1890s. Those who practice it are thrown out of the church. However, some small groups still stand by the practice. There are now thought to be about 30,000 polygamists in the western half of the United States.

Before Judge Guy Burningham decided on the sentence, Green's children sent letters pleading with him not to punish their father. From the letters it was clear that far from feeling badly treated by him, the children adored their father. "Please don't put our father in prison," wrote 10-year-old Lorin Green. One of Green's wives, Linda, told the judge that her husband's imprisonment would hurt the children. "Tom's children are very close to him," she wrote. "I believe they would suffer emotionally and mentally if he were taken away."

In addition to Green's family, a family doctor, school officials, and a scout leader all wrote letters of support to Judge Burningham.

Adapted from "US polygamist gets five years," BBC News Online, with permission. Copyright © 2001 BBC.

Reading Comprehension

Check Your Predictions

1. Look back at questions 1–4 in the Predict section. How accurate were your predictions?

Prediction	Not Accurate	Accurate
A. Reading 1		
A. Reading 2		
B. 1a		
B. 1b		
B. 1c		
B. 2		
B3. Reading 1		
B3. Reading 2		

2. If you found the answers to your questions, what were they?

Reading 1: _____

Reading 2: _____

Check the Facts

READING 1

A. Match the description and the corresponding statistic.

26%   38%   40%   45%   55%   56%   75%

_____ a. percentage of American adults that are married today

_____ b. percentage of American adults that were married 30 years ago

_____ c. percentage of married couples that have children today

_____ d. percentage of married couples that had children 30 years ago

_____ e. percentage of people who are happy with their first marriage

_____ f. percentage of couples who live together and then get married

_____ g. percentage of couples who live together and then break up after 5 years

B. Check (✓) the questions you can answer after reading once. Then go back and look for the answers that you are unsure of.

_____ 1. How is living together different today than it was 30 years ago?

_____ 2. Why does Robin Baker think that single parenthood will be normal in the twenty-first century?

READING 2

Check (✓) the questions you can answer after reading once. Then go back and look for the answers you are unsure of.

_____ 1. Where does Tom Green live?

_____ 2. How many years will he spend in prison?

_____ 3. What is the maximum sentence he could have received?

_____ 4. What was his defense?

_____ 5. Does the Mormon Church still allow polygamy?

_____ 6. Who wrote to the judge in Green's defense?

Analyze

Compare the relationships described in Reading 1 with Thomas Green's situation in Reading 2. How are they similar? How are they different?

Vocabulary Work

Guess Meaning from Context

1. Look for these words in the readings and guess their meanings.

Word/Phrase	Reading	Possible meaning or can probably ignore
proportion	1	_____
cohabitation	1	_____
prelude	1	_____
mobility	1	_____
in-vitro fertilization	1	_____
concurrent	2	_____
bigamy	2	_____
remote	2	_____
compound	2	_____
give up	2	_____
thrown out of	2	_____
pleading	2	_____

2. Grammar can sometimes help you guess the approximate meaning of unknown words. Read the example sentences. Are the words _opinionated_ and _obnoxious_ probably positive or negative. How do you know?

Everyone told me that Mike was very hardworking <u>but</u> opinionated.

Susie is very loud <u>and</u> obnoxious.

Guess if the <u>underlined</u> words are positive or negative.

> Is he <u>distressed</u> about this possibility? On the contrary, he's enthusiastic.

> From the letters it was clear that, far from feeling badly treated by him, they <u>adored</u> their father.

Guess Meaning from Related Words

1. Frequently, you will find different forms of the same word in one reading. These forms are usually related but have different suffixes. For example, you may find the verb *convict* and the noun *conviction*. Find other forms of these words in the readings.

   tradition _____

   increase _____

   sex _____

   possible _____

   polygamy _____

   prison _____

2. Work in pairs. Put the words from Exercise 1 in the correct columns. Compare your work with another pair when you are done.

Noun (person)	Noun (thing)	Verb	Adjective	Adverb

Reading Skills

Identifying Cohesive Words and Phrases

Cohesion *refers to the connections of ideas in a reading. Writers often use pronouns for cohesion, but they use other types of words and phrases, too. As a reader, it is important for you to be able to identify the cohesive elements and what they refer to.*

What does each <u>underlined</u> word refer to? Some words may have no referent.

1. In addition, a 1999 Rutgers University study reported that only 38 percent of Americans who are on their first marriages describe themselves as happy in <u>that state</u>.
2. <u>It</u>'s not that men and woman aren't interested in each other anymore.
3. Cohabitation used to be what people did before <u>they</u> got married.
4. Cohabitation is seen as a substitute for marriage rather than a prelude to <u>it</u>.
5. <u>This pattern</u> is redefining families.
6. Is he distressed about <u>this possibility</u>?
7. . . . four counts of bigamy and <u>one</u> of failing to pay child support.
8. He will not give <u>it</u> up even if <u>it</u> means going to prison.
9. <u>Those</u> who practice it are thrown out of the church.
10. However, some small groups still stand by <u>the practice.</u>

Discussion

1. Are children better raised in single-parent families, traditional two-parent families, or in polygamous families? Why?
2. What is your opinion of Robin Baker's predictions?
3. Do you agree with the judge's decision in the Thomas Green case? Why or why not?

PART II

This reading is more difficult than the articles in Part I. Read it for the main ideas. Do not worry if you cannot understand everything.

Read It

Read to find the answers to these questions.

1. What is the difference between Internet brides and picture brides?
2. Where do most mail-order brides come from today?
3. Where do many of their husbands come from?
4. How do men find brides on the Internet?
5. What qualities are many men looking for?
6. Does the writer believe that the mail-order bride business is racist? Why or why not?
7. What is the writer's opinion of the mail-order bride business? Why?

 READING

Mail-Order Brides— The Internet Revives an Old Tradition

During the first large wave of Asian immigration in the twentieth century, many Japanese and Korean women came to the United States as "picture brides." The picture-bride system, according to author Yen Le Espiritu, was a form of "arranged marriage facilitated by the exchange of photographs." A Japanese or Korean immigrant man would choose a wife based on a picture and send for her. The women agreed to become picture brides because, as one Korean woman put it, "then I could get to America . . . that land of freedom with streets paved with gold!"

In this century, picture brides have been replaced by mail-order brides. However, the two practices are different in an important

way. Korean and Japanese picture brides generally married men of the same ethnic group, whereas, in the mail-order bride system, men look for wives from countries other than their own. The homelands of modern mail-order brides also differ from those of yesterday's picture brides. Today, the majority come from the Philippines, Thailand, Latin America, and the former Soviet Union. Most of the men who "order" these women live in developed regions, such as Australia, North America, Western Europe, and Japan.

Each year, hundreds of Internet bride services recruit thousands of women— mostly from Eastern Europe, Southeast Asia, and other economically depressed

(Continued on next page)

parts of the globe—to marry their American clients. Matchmaking Web sites feature glowing testimonials and pictures of smiling couples. The sites promote old stereotypes of foreign women as subservient, "traditional" wives. For a large fee, the typical agency promises to connect clients with women who will "follow their husband's lead, and stick with the marriage even when times get tough and things stop being *fun*."

Many Internet brides settle into happy relationships; Encounters International claims a success rate of 86 percent, just 35 divorces out of 257 marriages. But Layli Miller-Muro, a lawyer who runs the Tahirih Justice Center, which is an international women's rights group, has followed problems in the foreign matchmaking industry for years. When she surveyed 175 legal-aid groups in the United States, more than half reported clients who had been mistreated by men they'd met through marriage brokers.

Some women claim that many men who want a mail-order bride simply want an obedient housekeeper and bed partner. And the agencies who sponsor the women "sell" them that way. For instance, one agency says that unlike modern-day American women, Filipinas are completely devoted to their husbands and families. Another Web site describes Latinas in the same way. Others depict Russian women as uncorrupted by the militant feminism that they say has ruined American women. An agency based in Italy states that Filipinas are still "good Catholic girls," implying that Italian women no longer are.

These agencies also don't paint a very pleasing picture of the men in women's native countries. For example, one says that Latin men get drunk and beat their wives. Another site says the same thing about Eastern European men. The purpose of this bad-mouthing is to convince clients that these women are grateful to marry a foreigner.

Some people say that the mail-order bride business is racist. However, that charge doesn't hold. A good portion of the brides are white, generally from the former Soviet Union, and some of the men who "order" brides are not. The movement of mail-order brides is less a flow of women from nonwhite to white countries than from poor to rich ones. The power of economics can be seen by looking at individual countries. When the mail-order bride business first caught the public's attention in the 1980s, most of the women were Asian. Yet a glance at any mail-order bride Web site shows virtually no women from Japan or Singapore. Japanese and Singaporean women don't need to go abroad as mail-order brides to improve their economic situation.

However, even if it is not racist, the mail-order bride business is not harmless. First of all, many women get involved in it because of unfavorable economic and/or social conditions in their homelands. Feminists and minority activists are also right to say that women who go abroad as wives of men whom they hardly know and who have such enormous economic and psychological power over them are easy targets for abuse.

Vocabulary Work

Guess Words from Context

1. Do you need to understand all of these words and phrases to answer the prereading questions? Cross out (~~word~~) the words that you can ignore. <u>Underline</u> the words you know. (Circle) the words you need to guess.

facilitated	ethnic	homelands	recruit	economically	depressed
clients	glowing	testimonials	stereotypes	matchmaking	
mistreated	flow	subservient	abuse	obedient	marriage brokers
feminism	militant	uncorrupted	ruined	devoted	unfavorable
pleasing	racist	virtually	harmless	bad-mouthing	

2. Read the clues below. Write the words and phrases from Exercise 1 under the clue that best helps you understand each one.

It looks like a word I know and/or I understood the prefix or suffix.

_____

I used my knowledge of marriage and marriage-related customs.

_____

I used my knowledge of psychology.

_____

I used logic.

_____

The writer gave a definition or explanation.

_____

Reading Skills

Understanding Advanced Punctuation

Sometimes writers use quotation marks to mark words that they are not using in their normal or literal sense.

How is the meaning of these words and phrases similar to but also different from their normal usage?

1. picture brides _____
2. order _____
3. traditional _____
4. sell _____

Idea Exchange

Think about Your Ideas

1. How are the following practices viewed in your society? Label each practice
    with the most appropriate term.

    encouraged   tolerated   condemned   outlawed   unheard of

    a. Cohabitation is _____ in my society.

    b. Serial monogamy is _____ in my society.

    c. Polygamy is _____ in my society.

    d. Mail-order brides are _____ in my society.

    e. Divorce is _____ in my society.

    f. Single parenthood is _____ in my society.

2. Which of these practices would you . . .

    personally tolerate or agree to?

    encourage a friend to do?

    encourage your sister or brother to do?

3. What, if any, practices in the list above should be against the law?

4. Who should regulate marriage—the government, religion, or communities?

Talk about Your Ideas

1. Is our society's conception of marriage changing? Why or why not?

2. Is traditional one man-one woman marriage important to society? If so,
    why? If not, why not?

For CNN video activities about a polygamist, turn to page 196.

CHAPTER 7

Prostitution: Looking for a good time?

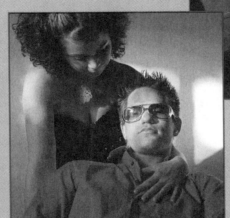

PREVIEW

Discuss these questions with your classmates.

1. Is prostitution illegal in your country? If so, what are the punishments?
2. Do you know the meaning of these words?

streetwalker	call girl	hooker	john
brothel	escort service	pimp	

PART I

Predict

A. Skim the readings and make predictions.

1. Which reading . . .

   a. probably comes from a newspaper?

   b. gives an opinion?

2. a. What is Ann Landers' opinion on prostitution?

   b. What does the letter writer want the government to do about prostitution?

   c. Does Reading 2 quote any people who do not support prostitution?

3. Predict the difficulty of each reading.

   a. Reading 1

   very easy   pretty easy   difficult   very difficult

   b. Reading 2

   very easy   pretty easy   difficult   very difficult

B. Write a question that you think each reading will answer.

Reading 1

_____

Reading 2

_____

Read It

Read the articles and look for the answers to your questions.

READING 1

A Prostitute Defends Her Chosen Profession

Dear Ann Landers:

A while back, you printed a letter about the dangers of prostitution. I would appreciate the opportunity to tell my side of the story. I hope you will print my letter because your assessment was not accurate.

I am a 31-year-old woman with a bachelor's degree from a well-known university. I have been a sex worker for the last 14 years and am happy with my career. It burns me up when I read studies that say we are messed-up drug addicts who were victims of child abuse or that we are at risk of getting beaten up or raped by our customers.

I do not deny that streetwalking is a difficult and stressful way to make a living, but not all prostitutes are streetwalkers. I work in a brothel in Nevada and would not trade my job for any other that I know of. I perform a valuable service that is legal in most counties in this state. Every woman who works out of our house gets checked by a doctor every week.

I have met some fascinating, successful, well-educated men through my profession. Many have been clients of mine for several years. I count among them doctors, lawyers, judges, college professors, politicians, and business executives. I make enough money working only two weeks each month and can use the other two weeks to pursue my writing career and work toward a Ph.D.

Ann, there's a reason prostitution is called "the world's oldest profession," and it isn't going away. Instead of fighting it, we should decriminalize it everywhere. For a woman who needs to feed her children, the threat of abuse is insignificant compared with watching her babies starve before her eyes. Legal sex work makes it possible for all women to have safer, stress-free working conditions. You should endorse it.

Magdalene at Madam Kitty's

Dear Magdalene:

I caught the significance of your name choice—from the Bible. It is obvious that you enjoy your work, and as I have said before, there always will be a market for what you are selling. For many years, I have been in favor of legalizing your profession and have said so. But please do not try to persuade anyone that babies would starve if their mothers did not go into prostitution. There are many other options—government assistance is the best known. I won't go down the list of others, but no woman in America needs to sell her body to make a living—unless, of course, she wants to.

Ann Landers

Excerpts from
Long Silent, Oldest Profession Gets Vocal and Organized
by Mireya Navarro, The New York Times

1 Shelby Aesthetic, a landscaper and writer in Huntsville, Ala., said she worked as a prostitute throughout her teenage years but never knew of a "sex workers movement" until last year, when she caught a performance of a touring art show where prostitutes performed and read short stories and poetry. "I had done sex work for years and I had never talked to anyone about it," Ms. Aesthetic, 25, said. "I didn't know there was anything out there." As often happens, a cultural interest opened doors to a social movement, this one involving "sex workers" and their supporters. In a new wave of activism, many prostitutes are organizing, staging public events and coming out publicly to demand greater acceptance and protection, giving a louder voice to a business that has thrived in silence. In Huntsville, Ms. Aesthetic—who says that is her real name—recently formed a chapter of the Sex Workers Outreach Project, a California group that itself was created from an organization in Australia last year, and is collecting statistics on prostitution arrests. At the Center for Sex and Culture in the hip South of Market area in San Francisco, prostitutes meet in support groups, hold fund-raisers and plot their next political move after having lost a ballot initiative in November that would have eased police enforcement of prostitution laws in Berkeley, Calif.

2   In New York, they are readying the first issue of a magazine for people in the sex industry for spring publication. And on the Internet, prostitutes have found a way not only to find customers but to find one another. They have formed online communities and have connected with groups in other countries. Despite the country's conservative climate, the ultimate goal for some in the movement is decriminalization, a move opposed by other former prostitutes who see the business as inherently exploitive and degrading. For now, though, the activists see ways to push ahead on goals shy of decriminalization, like stopping violence, improving working conditions, learning from foreign efforts to legimitze their work and taking some of the stigma off their trade. [. . .]

3   Prostitutes and their advocates say the illegal nature of their business makes them a target of violence because a majority of them do not report crimes for fear of being arrested or because they are ignored. "There are safe ways to work," says Carol Leigh, a longtime advocate for prostitutes' rights. "It's only a risk when it's illegal." Those who study prostitution say there is a wide range in types, from streetwalkers to high-priced call girls, and in the working conditions they face. [. . .]

4   Advocates of prostitute rights contend that it is a viable source of income for many women and that sexual activity between adults for money should be treated as any other form of legal labor. Ms. Few, 46, who is on probation for conspiring to promote prostitution, and others say their ultimate goal is to remove prostitution altogether from criminal codes, rather than confining it to legal brothels, as in Nevada. But opposition to that agenda is just as strong among many other prostitutes. Norma Hotaling, a former prostitute and founder of one of the best known groups working to help prostitutes leave

sex work, the SAGE Project in San Francisco, said that while giving prostitutes legal rights might help some women "build a business and make money," it would also feed into the worse consequences of commercial sex. [. . .]

5   But some of those working to help prostitutes leave their business see allies in those speaking out for sex workers. Celia Williamson, an assistant professor of social work at the University of Toledo in Ohio, said common ground could be found on calling public attention to the violence and lack of social services faced by streetwalkers, the most vulnerable of prostitutes. Ms. Williamson says her research shows that most of these women are victims of "sadistic and predatory" violence by customers, and scores suffer from drug addiction and mental illness. Last September, Ms. Williamson organized a conference to help spur a national strategy to deal with the problems. "Mostly we're sick and tired," said the social worker, who is chairwoman of the advisory board to an outreach program for prostitutes in Toledo. "Prostitution is like domestic violence 20 years ago. Nobody wants to talk about it. [. . .]

6   Few people predict that prostitutes are anywhere near obtaining legal rights, but some experts note that there are gains to be had if the movement perseveres.

Reading Comprehension

Check Your Predictions

1. Look back at questions 1–3 in the Predict section. How accurate were your predictions?

Prediction	Not Accurate	Accurate
1a		
1b		
2a		
2b		
2c		
3a		
3b		

2. If you found the answers to your questions, what were they?

Reading 1 _____

Reading 2 _____

Check the Facts

READING 1

Write T for *true*, F for *false*, or NS for *not sure*.

_____ 1. The letter writer is a prostitute.

_____ 2. The writer is uneducated.

_____ 3. The writer is not a streetwalker.

_____ 4. All prostitutes must see a doctor every week.

_____ 5. Prostitution is legal in the state of Nevada.

_____ 6. The writer believes that prostitution provides women with economic opportunities.

_____ 7. Ann Landers believes that poor women should become prostitutes.

READING 2

Check (✓) the questions you can answer after reading once. Then go back and look for the answers you are unsure of.

_____ 1. What is the world's oldest profession?

_____ 2. What kinds of activities are prostitutes organizing to do?

_____ 3. What is their final goal?

_____ 4. What are their intermediate or short-term goals?

_____ 5. Why do prostitutes say that they are the victims of violent crimes?

_____ 6. What is SAGE?

_____ 7. What problems do prostitutes have according to Celia Williamson?

_____ 8. What other social problems does she compare to prostitution?

Analyze

1. What are the similarities between the opinions given in Readings 1 and 2?

2. How is the situation of Magdalene in Reading 1 different from the situations described in Reading 2?

Vocabulary Work

Guess Meaning from Context

1. Look for these words in the readings. Guess their meanings or indicate if they can be ignored.

Word/Phrase	Reading	Possible meaning or ignore
assessment	1	_____
trade	1	_____
fascinating	1	_____
clients	1	_____
pursue	1	_____
starve	1	_____
options	1	_____
rights	2	_____
support groups	2	_____
labor	2	_____
ultimate	2	_____
advocate	2	_____
degrading	2	_____

2. Guess the meaning of these idioms.

my side of the story _____

burns me up _____

before her eyes _____

make a living _____

sick and tired _____

3. Use your knowledge of social problems to guess the meaning of these phrases.

support groups _____

drug addiction _____

mental illness _____

domestic violence _____

Guess Meaning from Related Words

*Often in a reading, you will find different forms of the same word. These words are usually related but have different **prefixes** or **suffixes**. For example, you may find the verb **organized** and the noun **organization**.*

1. Find other forms of the following words in the Readings.

criminal _____

legal _____

exploit _____

public _____

2. Work in pairs. Put the words from Exercise 1 in the correct columns. Compare your work with another pair when you are done.

Noun (person)	Noun (thing)	Verb	Adjective	Adverb

3. Sometimes we can recognize familiar words in compound words and phrases. Underline the familiar parts you recognize. Then guess the meaning of the words and phrases.

Word/Phrase	Meaning
messed up	_____
beaten up	_____
speak out	_____
open doors	_____
new wave	_____
longtime	_____

4. Look at the meanings of these prefixes. Then find at least two words in the readings that use them and guess their meanings.

Prefix	Meaning	Word(s)	Meaning
in-	not	_____	_____
		_____	
de-	against	_____	_____
		_____	

Reading Skills

Understanding Appositives

An **appositive** *is a phrase that means the same thing as a noun or gives further information about the noun.*

Find appositives for these nouns in the readings.

1. Shelby Aesthetic
2. a social movement
3. Norma Hotaling
4. Celia Williamson
5. the social worker

Discussion

1. Do you agree with Ann Landers' response to the letter writer? Why or why not?
2. Should prostitutes have legal rights? Why or why not?

PART II

This reading is more difficult than the articles in Part I. Read it for the main ideas. Do not worry if you cannot understand everything.

Read It

Read to find the answers to these questions.

1. Who is this story about?
2. Did she decide to become a prostitute?
3. Where was she sent?
4. What happened after she escaped?
5. How did she finally return home?
6. What is she doing now?
7. What does the writer think that the United States government should do?
8. What does Kristof compare sex trafficking with?

 (**READING**)

After the Brothel

by Nicholas D. Kristof, Op-Ed columnist, New York Times, 1/27/2005

1 POIPET, Cambodia—When I describe sex trafficking as, at its worst, a 21st-century version of slavery, I'm sure plenty of readers roll their eyes and assume that's hyperbole [that I am exaggerating]. It's true that many of the girls who are trafficked around the world go voluntarily, but then there are girls like Srey Rath.

2 A couple of years ago, at age 15 or 16 (she's unsure of her birth date), Srey Rath decided to go work in Thailand for two months so that she could give her mother a present for the Cambodian new year. But the work-traffickers who were supposed to get her and four female friends jobs as dishwashers smuggled them instead to Kuala Lumpur [Malaysia]. There, three of the girls, including Srey Rath, were locked up in a karaoke bar that was also a brothel. They were ordered to have sex with customers. Srey Rath indignantly resisted. "So the boss got angry and hit me in the face, first with one hand and then with the other," she remembers. "The mark stayed on my face for two weeks."

3 That was the beginning of a hell. The girls were forced to work in the brothel 15 hours a day, seven days a week, and they were never paid or allowed outside. Nor were they allowed to insist that customers use condoms. "They just gave us food to eat, but they didn't give us much because the customers didn't like fat girls," Srey Rath said.

4   The girls had been warned that if they tried to escape, they could be murdered. But they were so desperate that late one night, after they had been locked up in the 10th-floor apartment where they were housed, they pried a strong board off a rack used for drying clothes. Then they balanced the board, which was just 5 inches wide, from their window to a ledge in the next building, a dozen feet away.

5   Srey Rath and four other girls inched across, 10 floors above the pavement.

6   "We thought that even if we died, it would be better than staying behind," Srey Rath said. "If we stayed, we would die as well." (I talked to another of the Cambodians, Srey Hay, and she confirmed the entire account.)

7   Once on the other side, they took the elevator down and fled to a police station. But the police weren't interested and tried to shoo them away at first—and then arrested them for illegal immigration. Srey Rath spent a year in a Malaysian prison. When she was released, a Malaysian policeman drove her away and sold her to a taxi driver, who sold her to a Thai policeman, who sold her to a Thai brothel.

8   Finally, after two more months, Srey Rath fled again and made it home this time to her joyful family. An aid group, American Assistance for Cambodia, stepped in to help Srey Rath outfitting her with a street cart and an assortment of belts and keychains to sell. That cost only $400, and now she's thrilled to be earning money for her family.

9   Over the last five years, the United States has begun to combat sex trafficking, with President Bush's State Department taking the lead. But there's so much more that could be done particularly if the White House became involved. More scolding and shaming of countries with major sex trafficking problems, like Cambodia and Malaysia, would go a long way to get them to clean up their act.

10   . . .

11   You'll understand the importance of this if you ever cross the border between Thailand and Cambodia at Poipet: Look for a cart with a load of belts. You'll see a beaming teenage girl who will try to sell you a souvenir, and you'll realize that talk about sex "slavery" is not hyperbole [an exaggeration]—and that the shame lies not with the girls but with our own failure to respond as firmly to slavery today as our ancestors did in the 1860s.

Vocabulary Work

Guess Meaning from Context

1. Do you need to understand all of these words to answer the prereading questions? Cross out the (~~words~~) that you can ignore. Underline the words you know. Circle the words you need to guess.

sex trafficking	version	roll their eyes	hyperbole
locked up	resisted	hell	exaggerating
desperate	released	joyful	condoms
thrilled	combat	taking the lead	made it home
shaming	go a long way	clean up their act	scolding
beaming	firmly	ancestors	

2. Use the following kinds of clues to help you understand the words. Remember, it is often necessary to put several clues together in order to make a good guess. Write the word or phrase under the clue that helped you guess its meaning.

It looks like a word I know and/or I understood the prefix or suffix.

_____

_____

I used my world knowledge of this problem.

_____

_____

I used logic.

_____

_____

The writer gave a definition or explanation.

_____

_____

Reading Skills

Evaluating an Argument

Answer these questions.

1. What is Kristof's main argument?

_____

2. In which two paragraphs does he state his argument?

_____

3. What evidence does he use to support his argument?

_____

4. Is his argument effective?

_____

5. What other type of information, if any, would have made his argument stronger?

_____

6. Do you agree with him?

_____

Idea Exchange

Think about Your Ideas

1. What do you think are the three main causes of prostitution? Check (✓) the causes.

   _____ poverty

   _____ laziness

   _____ lack of education

   _____ sex trafficking

   _____ drug addiction

   _____ mental illness

   _____ lack of good job opportunities for women

   _____ other _____

2. Are there any arguments for decriminalizing prostitution that you agree with? What are they?

3. Are there any arguments for keeping prostitution illegal that you agree with? What are they?

Talk about Your Ideas

1. Is prostitution a major social problem? If so, why? If not, why not?

2. Should prostitution be legalized? Give reasons for your opinion.

3. Would legalization of prostitution affect sex trafficking or would it make no difference?

For CNN video activities about the social impact of prostitution, turn to page 197.

CHAPTER 8

Education: Is *everyone* cheating?

PREVIEW

Read the following article. Discuss it with your classmates.

Gypsum, Colo.—A high school graduate has confessed to cheating on an English literature test—47 years ago. High school principal Mark Strakbein said he got a one-page, handwritten letter from a 65-year-old grandmother who admitted she and a friend stole the answers to a Shakespeare test in the fall of 1957.

"I know it makes no difference now (after 47 years), except maybe this will keep some students from cheating and help them to be honest—conscience never lets you forget—there is forgiveness with God, and I have that, but I felt I still needed to confess to the school."

Strakbein said he read the letter aloud to every homeroom class as a lesson in following your conscience.

"You could have heard a pin drop," he said.

PART I

Predict

A. Skim the readings and make predictions.

1. Where did each reading come from? Why do you think so?
   a. a newspaper
   b. a magazine
   c. an encyclopedia

2. Which reading . . .
   a. gives advice?
   b. reports on a problem?
   c. gives an opinion?

3. Skim the readings. Which one . . .
   a. includes statistics?
   b. gives real-life example/s?
   c. talks about high school students?
   d. is probably written by a journalist?

4. Predict the difficulty of each reading.
   a. Reading 1
      very easy   pretty easy   difficult   very difficult
   b. Reading 2
      very easy   pretty easy   difficult   very difficult

B. Write a question that you think each reading will answer.

Reading 1

_____

Reading 2

_____

Read It

Read the articles and look for the answers to your questions.

 (**READING 1**)

The Whys and Hows of Cheating

Why Students Do It—How We Can Stop Them

1   The first thing to understand about cheating is that the vast majority of young people believe that cheating is wrong. Yet surveys show that most young people cheat at least once in their high school careers. So, the most important question is why do young people behave in ways that are inconsistent with their beliefs? According to Gary Niels, an educator who has studied cheating in our schools, the answer is survival. In a school setting, says Niels, saving face is the, ". . . desire to save oneself from the anger of a parent or teacher; it can mean avoiding embarrassment; it can mean economic survival . . . Nowadays, college acceptance is the major instigator of this survival instinct." There's a lot of competition to get accepted at the best schools. Acceptance at these elite colleges and universities requires great grades—so if you can't do the work, you have to be dishonest and cheat. In addition, many students feel that everyone else is cheating, so they'll be at a disadvantage if they don't cheat.

What to Do about It? Combating Cheating at Home

2   Of course, it is easy to point the finger at young people and say that they are immoral. However, who is supposed to give them their moral compass? We are. Somehow our society has grown to tolerate cheating and it has been a top-down rather than a bottom-up process. Children learn to cheat or at least cut corners at home from their parents. Many of them are not taught to see the difference between right and wrong. Other children hear the right lessons, but observe their parents behaving very differently. Parents need to model integrity at all times. Consider this simple example:

> Last night I was attending a movie with my family. My son ran into a classmate whose father was in the next ticket line. When we reached the front of the line to buy our tickets, we all heard the boy's father say "One adult, two children" to the ticket agent. Although his son was too old for a child's ticket, he decided that he could get away with it. He saved a couple of dollars and taught his son a terrible lesson.

Combating Cheating at School

3   Yes, it's disturbing to discover that young people in middle school and high school think that cheating is OK. But it's our fault. We encourage young people to cheat! For example, we give multiple-choice tests that make cheating really easy. Teachers at academically rigorous private schools don't use multiple-choice tests. They create written tests that are more work for teachers to grade but that eliminate cheating.

4   Schools should not tolerate cheating in any form. The punishments should be rigorously enforced. Teachers must be alert to all forms of cheating, particularly those using new technologies like picture phones. Of course, the best solution is to make assignments meaningful and interesting for students. In addition, students must have some responsibility. They must learn to be true to themselves and their own values and not be swayed by outside pressures and influences.

READING 2

More Students Are Cheating, More Colleges Are Fighting Back

1 BOSTON—Many college students today struggle with cheating. The Internet offers many temptations—there are term papers for sale along with articles and news reports that can be copied for free with the click of a mouse. It is not surprising that cheating is sometimes difficult to resist. Furthermore, students often do not understand exactly what constitutes cheating. Polly Sanders, a student at a small liberal arts college, knows that handing in a paper from the Internet is plagiarism—stealing another's writing and calling it your own. If she gets caught, she'll receive a failing grade or maybe be thrown out of school. But what about using a paragraph? She admits that she has often taken a paragraph and changed a few words to make it "her" own work. That's not plagiarizing, is it? Polly may not know it but, according to her college, it is.

2 Polly is not the only student who isn't sure what's cheating and what isn't. This uncertainty is partly due to the fact that standards are changing. A 2001 survey by the Center for Academic Integrity shows cheating is becoming acceptable. The survey found that 41 percent of students believe that plagiarism is common. Thirty percent say cheating during tests or exams happens quite often. Sixty percent of the students admit asking their friends for help even when a professor has told them to work alone. Perhaps most worrying was the 27 percent who said that falsifying laboratory data happens "often or very often" on campus. It's hard to believe that all of these young scientists change their ways after graduation. Especially since 45 percent said that falsifying data did not count as serious cheating.

3 If students are becoming less concerned about the ramifications of cheating, colleges and universities are working harder to catch the cheaters. Some administrators use sophisticated computer search engines to find Internet plagiarists. However, many other colleges are using honor codes to combat cheating. An effective honor code clearly describes the boundaries of legitimate and illegitimate work. In addition, it sets the penalties for breaking it. While honor codes have existed on many campuses for a long time, they are now acquiring "teeth" as the institutions strive to enforce them. Educators say that the simple act of students signing the honor code makes a difference. "It's a psychological effect: if people expect you to be honorable, you are more likely to respond with honorable behavior," says Nannerl O. Keohane, the president of Duke University in North Carolina. "We have to build a culture where people are genuinely offended by cheating."*

4   Honor codes are becoming more and more popular across the United States. The University of North Carolina and the University of Maryland give cheaters grades of XF to indicate failure because of cheating. Cornell University rewrote its honor code in 2000 and now requires teaching assistants and freshmen to take courses that teach them what cheating is and how to avoid it.

5   Honor codes can be both a carrot and a stick. They may offer students more freedom, but, if they do not obey, the punishment is severe. For example, the honor code at Wellesley College in Massachusetts allows students to take exams when and where they want. The students simply inform the teacher when they will be taking the exam. Then they can choose to go wherever they want. Some stay in the classroom while others prefer to do exams in their bedrooms, the library, or outside. The students are trusted, but if they are caught cheating, the punishment can be severe.

6   Some people say that simply putting in an honor code won't solve the problem, but several studies since the 1960s have shown that schools without honor codes tend to have about twice as much cheating as those with honor codes in place. University officials think that there are different reasons for this phenomenon. "The feeling of being treated as an adult and responding in kind," Professor McCabe says, "it's clearly there for many students. They don't want to violate that trust."* "The magic of an honor code," agrees Elizabeth Kiss, director of the Kenan Institute for Ethics at Duke University, "is that when it's really working, there's a sense of we're all in this together."

*Source: Zermke, Kate. "With Student Cheating on the Rise, More Colleges Are Turning to Honor Codes," New York Times (online) (November 2, 2002).

Reading Comprehension

Check Your Predictions

1. Look back at questions 1–4 in the Predict section. How accurate were your predictions?

Prediction	Not Accurate	Accurate
1a		
1b		
1c		
2a		
2b		
2c		
3a		
3b		
3c		
3d		
4a		
4b		

2. If you found the answers to your questions, what were they?

Reading 1

_____

Reading 2

_____

Check the Facts

READING 1

Write T for *true,* **F for** *false,* **or NS for** *not sure.*

According to Reading 1 . . .

_____ 1. Most students think that cheating is wrong.

_____ 2. Students cheat because it's a challenge.

_____ 3. Students are very worried about getting into college.

_____ 4. Students cheat even though their parents teach them not to.

_____ 5. Teachers shouldn't give multiple-choice tests.

_____ 6. Cheaters should not be punished too severely.

_____ 7. Some students cheat using picture phones.

READING 2

Check (✓) the questions you can answer after reading once. Then go back and look for the answers you are unsure of.

_____ 1. How can students cheat using the Internet?

_____ 2. Are students confused about cheating? Why?

_____ 3. What does the group represented by each percentage believe about cheating?

41%   30%   60%   27%   45%

_____ 4. What is the purpose of an honor code?

_____ 5. How is each college or university handling cheating?
- Duke University
- University of Maryland
- Cornell University
- Wellesley College

_____ 6. Do honor codes reduce cheating? Why or why not?

Analyze

1. Compare the attitudes of the university officials quoted in Reading 2 with the writer of Reading 1.

2. Would the solutions to cheating stated in Reading 1 work at a college or university? Why or why not?

Vocabulary Work

Guess Meaning from Context

1. Look for these words in the readings. Guess their meanings.

Word	Reading	Meaning
vast	1	_____
surveys	1	_____
inconsistent	1	_____
integrity	1	_____
multiple-choice	1	_____
rigorous	1	_____
tolerate	1	_____
struggle	2	_____
temptations	2	_____
resist	2	_____
plagiarism	2	_____
standards	2	_____
strive	2	_____
combat	2	_____

- A **metaphor** *suggests a similarity between one thing and another.*
- An **idiom** *is an expression that does not mean the same as the individual words.*
- A **colloquial expression** *is informal language.*

2. The expressions below are found in the reading. Can you guess the meaning of these *metaphors*, *idioms*, and *colloquial expressions?*

READING 1

saving face	_____
point the finger	_____
moral compass	_____
top-down/bottom-up	_____
cut corners	_____

READING 2

with the click of a mouse	_____
get away with	_____
"teeth"	_____
make a difference	_____
a carrot and a stick	_____

Guess Meaning from Related Words

1. Sometimes we can recognize that words are related to words that we already know. Find words in the readings that are related to these.

embarrass   _____

survive   _____

compete   _____

academic   _____

rigor   _____

false   _____

honor   _____

accept   _____

cheat   _____

2. Work in pairs. Put the words from Exercise 1 in the correct columns. Compare your work with another pair when you are done.

Noun (person)	Noun (thing)	Verb	Adjective	Adverb

3. Look at the meanings of these prefixes. Then look for the words that use them in the readings and guess their meanings.

Prefix	Meaning	Word(s)	Meaning
il-	not	_____	_____
im-	not	_____	_____
dis-	not	_____	_____
		_____	_____

Reading Skills

Finding Main Ideas in Topic Sentences

The main idea in a paragraph is given in the topic sentence. Often the topic sentence is the first sentence in the paragraph, but it doesn't have to be. Look back at Readings 1 and 2. Underline the topic sentences. Then paraphrase the main idea and write it below.

Reading 1	Sentence Number	Main Idea
Paragraph 1	_____	_____
Paragraph 2	_____	_____
Paragraph 3	_____	_____
Paragraph 4	_____	_____

Reading 2	Sentence Number	Main Idea
Paragraph 1	_____	_____
Paragraph 2	_____	_____
Paragraph 3	_____	_____
Paragraph 4	_____	_____
Paragraph 5	_____	_____
Paragraph 6	_____	_____

Discussion

1. Does your school have an honor code? If so, is it effective?
2. What happens to cheaters at your school? Is the punishment consistent?

PART II

This reading is more difficult than the articles in Part I. Read it for the main ideas. Do not worry if you cannot understand everything.

Read It

Read to find the answers to these questions.

1. What was the writer's job in college?
2. Did he come from a wealthy family?
3. What did he see in the mailboxes every week?
4. Why was this such a temptation?
5. What reasons did he think of for stealing the answers?
6. What did he do in the end? Why?
7. How does he feel about his decision? Why?

 READING

The Economics of Cheating
by Carlos Lozada

As a college student, I worked 15 hours a week at a university research institute. The job was fun, but I worked out of necessity. School was expensive, and the extra income was a must.

One day a week I put notices in the mailboxes of dozens of professors. One afternoon, as I was stuffing the mailboxes in the economics department, I noticed a large stack of papers in the mailbox of one of my instructors. The top sheet read "Answer Key: ECON 303 Problem Set."

Economics 303 (ECON 303) was my toughest class that semester. It covered statistics and introductory econometrics. The problem sets were very time-consuming. Looking at the stack, I saw how easily I could take a copy off the top. No one would see me. I was totally alone. In the end, I didn't take a copy. Instead, I stayed up late that night finishing the problem set. In class the next day I handed the assignment in and received the same answer sheet I'd seen the day before. With a deep sigh, I reviewed my mistakes.

(Continued on next page)

Resisting temptation became a weekly ritual. The papers called to me every week. There were so many copies of the answer key that I knew no one would notice if I took one. As the assignments became more difficult, it became more and more difficult to walk away.

I began thinking of reasons for taking a copy. The detailed answer sheet would be a great learning tool—a study aid, really. I wouldn't stop doing the homework. I would simply look at the answers if I got stuck. I'd save time. It would even help the poor, overworked teaching assistant who had to figure out my errors. How selfless of me!

The semester grew more intense. Classes, work at the institute, singing rehearsals, my girlfriend, those insufferable problem sets—I began feeling overwhelmed by all these commitments. I finally decided to take an answer key. I remember walking into the economics mailroom, half hoping the papers wouldn't be there. But there they were as always, and as always there was no one around. All I had to do was take the top copy and put it into my book bag.

But I stood there, thinking about the consequences. Of course, there was the honor code I'd signed. But more disturbing to me was the possibility I could be caught. Maybe the copies were numbered. Perhaps a classmate would find out. Was it worth it? Was saving myself a few hours of work worth the risk of suspension or expulsion? Calculating the costs and benefits, I decided I'd worked too hard to throw everything away on something like this. The benefit would be small, and the possible downside enormous. I walked away.

Seven years later, my college diploma now sits atop a cluttered bookshelf in my living room. It's one of the first things I see when I walk in the door, and a source of great pride. I wonder: Would I look upon it differently if I had taken the answer key? Maybe I would. My achievement would be diminished, my pride qualified. Perhaps most important, the sacrifices my family made so I could attend a first-tier university would be betrayed.

But I can't congratulate myself too much because my decision was based on fear as well as principle. Does the motivation matter? Or does it still count as "doing the right thing" when you do it for the wrong reasons?

Vocabulary Work

Guess Meaning from Context

1. Do you need to understand all of these words to answer the prereading questions? Cross out (~~words~~) the words that you can ignore. <u>Underline</u> the words you know. (Circle) the words you need to guess.

a must	overworked	expulsion	sigh	diminished
assignments	suspension	econometrics	qualified	insufferable
consequences	stack	overwhelmed	cluttered	first-tier
stuffing	selfless	atop		

2. Guess the meaning of the words you circled. What clues did you use? Write each word under the clue that helped you guess its meaning.

It looks like a word I know.

_____

I guessed from an example.

_____

I used my knowledge of the world.

_____

I understood the prefix.

_____

There is a definition or a synonym in the reading.

_____

Reading Skills

Summarizing a Narrative

When you **summarize** *a story, you include only the most important parts. In other words, summaries usually concentrate on action and leave out description.*

Reread Carlos Lozada's narrative. Write a summary including one sentence for every paragraph. Compare your summary with a partner's. How are they similar? How are they different?

_____

_____

_____

_____

_____

_____

_____

_____

_____

Idea Exchange

Think about Your Ideas

Number each action from 1 to 10—One being the least dishonest and 10 being the most dishonest.

_____ Helping a friend with homework.

_____ Helping a friend on a test.

_____ Taking a paragraph or two from the Internet and inserting it into your work.

_____ Writing test answers on your arm.

_____ Looking at a friend's paper during an exam.

_____ Buying a paper from an essay service on the Internet.

_____ Stealing a test from your teacher's drawer.

_____ Asking a friend to edit an essay for you.

_____ Borrowing an old test from a student who took the course last year.

_____ Talking to a friend about your answers on a take-home test.

Talk about Your Ideas

Compile the class opinions from the survey above. Discuss the results.

For CNN video activities about the effects of cheating in school, turn to page 198.

CHAPTER 9

Gender:
Are women weak?
Are men necessary?

PREVIEW

Discuss these questions with your classmates.

1. Look at this list of jobs. Is there any job that one sex should not be allowed to do? Is there any job that one sex can do better than the other? Give reasons for your opinions.

fashion model	lawyer	poet
construction worker	mathematician	police officer
dancer	nurse	president or prime minister
engineer	nursery-school teacher	business executive
firefighter	pilot	wrestler
basketball coach		

2. List other jobs that you think are better suited to a specific gender. Do your classmates agree? Ask for the reasons behind their opinions.

_____   _____
_____   _____
_____   _____
_____   _____

PART I

Predict

A. Skim the readings and make predictions.

1. Which reading . . .

   a. probably states an opinion?

   b. explains a scientific study?

2. Does Reading 2 attack or defend Lawrence Summers?

3. Does the writer of Reading 1 have a generally positive or negative view of the military?

4. Predict the difficulty of each reading.

   a. Reading 1

   very easy   pretty easy   difficult   very difficult

   b. Reading 2

   very easy   pretty easy   difficult   very difficult

B. Write a question that you think each reading will answer.

Reading 1

_____

Reading 2

_____

Read It

Read the articles and look for the answers to your questions.

READING 1

Are Women Strong Enough for Combat? You Bet!

American women have made terrific gains toward equality in many ways. However, there is one glaring exception—the military. The armed services allow women to join but will not allow them to fight. When one considers the evidence with an open mind, there is absolutely no intelligent reason for women not to be in combat roles. There are political, patriarchal, religious, and misogynistic reasons but no logical reasons. Still, the old-fashioned concepts that fill the closed minds of the "brotherhood of the sword,"— the military establishment—can be heard everywhere from the Congress to the media.

One of the main reasons the military establishment gives for not allowing women to fight concerns physical strength. Military officials claim that women are just not strong enough to undergo the rigors of combat. That argument has now been disproven. The army's own researchers published a study that concludes that when a woman is correctly trained, she can be as tough as any man. The report by the U.S. Army Research Institute of Environmental Medicine was led by Everett Harman. "You don't need testosterone (the male sex hormone) to get strong," Harman concluded. Through a regimen of regular jogging, weight training, and other rigorous exercise, more than 75 percent of the 41 women in the study were able to prepare themselves to successfully carry out duties traditionally performed by males in the military. Before training, less than 25 percent of the women were capable of performing the tasks. All but one of the females were civilian volunteers—a group that included lawyers, mothers, students, and bartenders. None of the volunteers were used to strenuous physical activity. Several had recently had children.

The 24-week training study began in May, 1995. All the women spent 90 minutes a day, five days a week, building themselves up for endurance tests. They ran a two-mile course wearing a 75-pound backpack and performed squats thrusts with a 100-pound barbell on their shoulders. The volunteers showed more than a 33 percent improvement in physical strength and endurance. At the same time, the Ministry of Defense in Great Britain ran the same kind of study. The *Sunday Times* of London reported that "by using new methods of physical training, women can be built up to the same levels of physical fitness as men of the same size and build." The article also notes that "contrary to the view of many traditionalists, the performance of groups improve greatly if both sexes are involved."

Today, over 200,000 women serve in the armed forces, comprising more than 17 percent of the total force. About 80 percent of the jobs and more than 90 percent of the career fields are open to women. The pure and simple point is that all jobs should be open to women and men if—and only if—the women and men are qualified, capable, competent, and able to perform them! Nothing more, nothing less.

Questions That One Isn't Allowed to Ask

Recently, Lawrence Summers, the president of Harvard University, got himself into a lot of hot water. Summers, who was trained as an economist, was speaking at a seminar for scientists. He had not written a speech; he spoke only from notes. His comments were supposed to be off the record. His topic was why there are not more women at the highest levels in science. Women make up 35 percent of the faculty in U.S. higher education. Furthermore, female students outnumber male students. However, they hold only 20 percent of the top positions in science. Summers warned his audience that his remarks would probably cause debate.

First, he admitted that there was undoubtedly prejudice in the hiring of women in university science departments. However, he said that he felt this was not the main reason that there were so few women in the top jobs. He felt that the fact that some female scientists choose to spend critical research years at home with their children was another important factor. This comment was only mildly controversial. Then he moved on to much more dangerous territory. He mentioned research by the University of Michigan sociologist Yu Xie and his University of California-Davis colleague, Kimberlee A. Shauman. Xie and Shauman were studying why, although the median or average score for men and women was roughly the same in science tests, there were many more men at the very bottom and at the very top of the range. Summers stated that one possible explanation for this discrepancy is genetics. He immediately added, "I'd like to be proven wrong on this one."

At that point, Professor Nancy Hopkins, a biology professor from the Massachusetts Institute of Technology (MIT), walked out. She later told the *New York Times* that she was offended by Summers' comments. "When he started talking about inborn differences in aptitude between men and women, I just couldn't breathe because this kind of bias makes me physically ill. Let's not forget that people used to say that women couldn't drive an automobile."

How can anyone who calls herself a scientist have such an emotional reaction to a scientific question? As Steven Pinker, also from MIT, said, "Look, the truth cannot be offensive. Perhaps the hypothesis is wrong, but how would we ever find out whether it is wrong if it is 'offensive' even to consider it? People who storm out of a meeting at the mention of a hypothesis, or declare it taboo or offensive without providing arguments or evidence, don't get the concept of a university or free inquiry."

Is Summers' question ridiculous? Not at all. Every day scientists are discovering more and more about the differences between male and female brains. One thing that is common across all populations and cultures is that males score better in tests of spatial and mathematical reasoning. Have you ever wondered why boys are more likely to be autistic? The cause is much more likely genetic than environmental.

(Continued on next page)

Scientists have also discovered connections between certain behavioral traits and levels of testosterone. Both men and women have testosterone, but men have a lot more. Among testosterone-related characteristics are aggression, lack of focus, and edginess. Everyone accepts that 95 percent of all hyperactive kids are boys or that four times as many boys have learning disabilities. Science has also shown that boys have a greater difference between their right and left brains and worse linguistic skills. These are generalizations, of course. Many males are great linguists and model students, just as many women are great scientists and mathematicians.

Of course, it is difficult to talk about innate inequality. However, everyone accepts that people have varying degrees of intelligence, musical talent, and mathematical abilities. When Thomas Jefferson wrote, "All men are created equal," he didn't mean equal in ability. He was referring to political equality. Anything that science discovers about human nature should never be used to deny opportunities to different groups of people, nor should the desire for equality obstruct legitimate scientific inquiry and debate.

Adapted from "The Truth about men and women is too hot to handle" by Andrew Sullivan, with permission. Copyright © 2005 The Sunday Times, London.

Reading Comprehension

Check Your Predictions

1. Look back at questions 1–4 in the Predict section. How accurate were your predictions?

Prediction	Not Accurate	Accurate
1a		
1b		
2		
3		
4a		
4b		

2. If you found the answers to your questions, what were they?

Reading 1

_____

Reading 2

_____

Check the Facts

(**READING 1**)

Write T for *true,* **F for** *false,* **or NS for** *not sure.*

_____ 1. Women are only able to participate in combat in unusual situations.

_____ 2. Many people in the U.S. Congress and the media believe women should be able to fight.

_____ 3. Studies show that all women are as strong as men.

_____ 4. Women do not have testosterone.

_____ 5. The American study used women from the military.

_____ 6. The British researchers came up with a different conclusion than the Americans.

_____ 7. Less than 20 percent of the military is made up of women.

_____ 8. Women have 80 percent of the jobs in the military.

(**READING 2**)

A. Check (✓) the questions you can answer after reading once. Then go back and look for the answers you are unsure of.

_____ 1. What was Lawrence Summers's topic?

_____ 2. What two reasons did Summer give for his argument?

_____ 3. Who walked out and why?

_____ 4. Does Steven Pinker agree with Nancy Hopkins? Why or why not?

_____ 5. How does the author feel about Summers's comments?

_____ 6. Name some differences that science has found in male and female brains.

_____ 7. Does the writer believe that people are born equal in ability? Why or why not?

B. Which of these statements would the writer probably agree with? Check (✓) those sentences.

_____ 1. Women should not be scientists.

_____ 2. A male scientist is always better than a female scientist.

_____ 3. Fewer women than men are naturally good at science.

Analyze

1. Are the conclusions of the writers of Readings 1 and 2 compatible, incompatible, or totally unconnected? Why?

2. Summers said that prejudice contributed to the lack of female scientists. According to the arguments of the writer in Reading 1, is the military also prejudiced against women?

Vocabulary Work

Guess Meaning from Context

Look for these words in the readings. Guess their meanings.

Word	Reading	Meaning
glaring	1	_____
combat	1	_____
media	1	_____
concludes	1	_____
tough	1	_____
regimen	1	_____
civilian	1	_____
endurance	1	_____
contrary	1	_____
faculty	2	_____
debate	2	_____
bias	2	_____
hypothesis	2	_____
taboo	2	_____
traits	2	_____
innate	2	_____

Guess Meaning from Related Words

1. Guess the meaning of these idioms from the readings.

open mind _____

closed mind _____

brotherhood of the sword _____

get into hot water _____

off the record _____

2. Underline the common words in these compound words and phrases. Then guess their meanings.

undergo _____

carry out _____

3. Find other forms of these words in the readings.

rigor _____

aggressive _____

edgy _____

generalize _____

behavior _____

doubt _____

gene _____

4. Work in pairs. Put the words from exercises 2 and 3 in the correct columns. Compare your work with another pair when you are done.

Noun (person)	Noun (thing)	Verb	Adjective	Adverb

5. Look at the meanings of these prefixes. Then look for the words that use them in the readings, and guess their meanings.

Prefix	Meaning	Word(s)	Meaning
dis-	not	_____	_____
		_____	_____
		_____	_____
hyper-	above, away	_____	_____
in-	in, within	_____	_____
		_____	_____
		_____	_____
		_____	_____
		_____	_____

Reading Skills

Identifying Main Ideas and Supporting Details

The purpose of both articles is to persuade their audience. Writers often use **supporting details** *to convince readers that their point of view is correct. There are a number of different types of supporting details. Some of the most common ones are:*

statistics

quotations from experts

logic

citations from scientific studies

examples

1. What is the author of Reading 1 trying to persuade readers to believe?
2. What kinds of supporting details does she use?
3. What is the main argument of the writer of Reading 2?
4. What kinds of supporting details does he use?

Discussion

1. Do you agree with the writer of Reading 1? Why or why not?
2. Do you agree with the writer of Reading 2? Why or why not?

PART II

This reading is more difficult than the articles in Part I. Read it for the main ideas. Do not worry if you cannot understand everything.

Read It

Read to find the answers to these questions.

1. What two types of problems may face males in the future?
2. What chromosome combination produces a female? a male?
3. What has been happening to the Y chromosome?
4. Why is this a problem?
5. Do all scientists agree that the Y chromosome is in trouble?
6. What has Dr. George Daley produced in a laboratory?
7. What is asexual reproduction?

 READING

The End of Sex?

All of the arguments about men's and women's roles and abilities may be irrelevant in the future. Why? Because some scientists believe that in a few hundred years, there might not even be two sexes. How is that possible? It may sound silly, but there is reason to fear that the "stronger" sex is in danger of extinction. Indeed, males are in danger on two fronts. The first is genetic and the other technological.

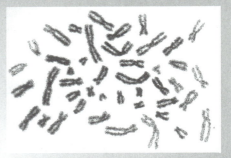

X and Y chromosomes

An endangered chromosome?

You are probably thinking that only men can make sperm, and sperm is required for human reproduction. Thus, men must be essential to the future of our species. Unfortunately, scientists are finding that this may not be the case. In order to understand why, you need to understand some basic genetics.

Each of our cells contains 23 pairs of chromosomes. Twenty-two of these pairs are matched pairs shared by men and women. The twenty-third is different. In women, the twenty-third pair is made up of two X chromosomes. In men, it has an X chromosome and a Y chromosome. That Y chromosome holds genes necessary for forming male sex organs and making sperm.

It turns out that not having an identical match is problematic for the Y chromosome. Why? Because every time a cell divides, it is at risk for a genetic mistake or a mutation to occur. In paired chromosomes, this generally is not a problem because if a gene on one chromosome is damaged, a cell can get the correct genetic information from the other chromosome.

The Y chromosome does not have this back-up system. So when a gene on the Y chromosome goes bad, it disappears. Scientists believe that the X and Y chromosomes probably started with about 1,000 genes. Today the Y chromosome has fewer than 80. Because of this problem, some geneticists believe that the Y chromosome will eventually disappear. If that happens, it will be the end of sexual reproduction. However, not everyone is so pessimistic about the Y chromosome's chances of survival. David Page of MIT's Whitehead Institute says, "At the same time that it is continuing to lose genes, it [the Y chromosome] has found some new ways of replenishing or rebuilding itself."

There is reason to believe he may be correct. Last year, Page and his colleagues reported that the Y chromosome has been secretly creating back-up copies of its most important genes. These are stored as mirror images or palindromes, which have the ability to read the same way forwards and backwards. In these genetic palindromes, the first half contains the gene and the second half contains the same information, just in reverse. That means that the Y chromosome has actually made a copy of itself that allows it to repair damaged genes.

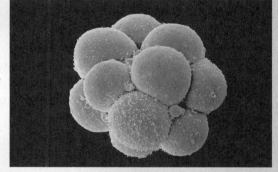

An early embryo called a blastocyst

Test-tube sperm?

However, even if the Y chromosome escapes genetic extinction, males face another threat from a technology that scientists are creating. Everyone agrees that sperm are necessary for sexual reproduction, but what if men were not necessary to make sperm? What if sperm could be made in a laboratory?

Last year, Dr. George Daley and his colleagues at Children's Hospital in Boston did just that. They proved that they could not only create sperm in a laboratory but also use that sperm to fertilize a mouse egg. The fertilized eggs then developed into early embryos called blastocysts.

Of course, scientists do not know whether these laboratory sperm will be able to do everything that normal sperm can do. In addition, they haven't shown that mouse embryos created by these sperm would grow into mice. However, Daley is confident that they will be able to do just that.

Daley and his fellow scientists say that they are not trying to make men unnecessary. They are simply trying to learn more about sperm cell development and infertility. He also points out that men are still indispensable because to make a sperm cell you need a Y chromosome and that must come from a man. However, while it is true that you need a Y chromosome to start, once stem cells begin making sperm, they can continue doing it forever.

(Continued on next page)

No sperm at all?

As if all of the above evidence that males may not be necessary for reproduction were not enough, some scientists are experimenting with parthenogenetic reproduction. In this type of reproduction, no sperm are necessary. The egg simply divides to create an embryo. Some reptiles, amphibians, and insects have the ability to reproduce in this way, but mammals do not. However, in 2004, Japanese scientists found a way to make unfertilized mouse eggs reproduce themselves. The procedure was complex and not very reliable. Out of 457 eggs, only eight mice were born. But the fact that it worked at all was unexpected. It showed that it was possible for mammals to reproduce asexually.

So, while there is no need for men to worry any time soon, in the future the male sex faces challenges on a number of fronts.

Adapted from "The End of Men?" Parts I and II, with permission. Copyright © 2004 National Public Radio

Vocabulary Work

Guess Meaning from Context

1. Do you need to understand all of these words to answer the prereading questions? Cross out (~~word~~) the words that you can ignore. <u>Underline</u> the words you know. (Circle) the words you need to guess.

irrelevant	extinction	essential	species
problematic	mutation	paired	back-up
pessimistic	replenishing	geneticists	matched
palindromes	threat	blastocysts	

2. Use the following kinds of clues to help you understand the words from Exercise 1. Remember, it is often necessary to put several clues together in order to make a good guess. Write the word or phrase under the clue that helped you guess each word's meaning.

   It looks like a word I know and/or I understood the prefix or suffix.

   _____

   I used my knowledge of reproduction and genetics.

   _____

   I used logic.

   _____

   The writer gave a definition or explanation.

   _____

Reading Skills

Understanding Organization

You will read much more effectively if you understand the organization of what you are reading. Sometimes readings are organized in a linear fashion. Others have larger ideas that contain a number of other ideas.

In your notebook, complete this outline of the reading: "The End of Sex."

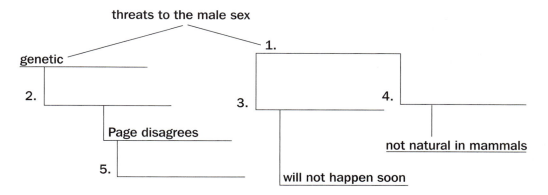

Idea Exchange

Think about Your Ideas

For each statement below, decide how you feel and write the number. Think of reasons for your opinions.

1	2	3	4	5
agree strongly	agree	aren't sure	disagree	disagree strongly

_____ a. Science is going to show us that men and women are much more alike than most people think.

_____ b. In the future, we are likely to discover that men and women are more different than we had ever imagined.

_____ c. Most differences between men and women are innate.

_____ d. In a perfect society, men and women would be raised exactly the same.

_____ e. It doesn't matter what science discovers about the nature of men and women; both sexes should still be offered the same opportunities.

_____ f. Society is right to discriminate. Policies should be made to benefit the average person not the unusual person.

_____ g. Talking about general differences between the sexes is useless. Each person should be judged as an individual.

Talk About Your Ideas

1. Take a poll of the class. Which statements did most people agree with most strongly? Why?

2. Which statements did most people disagree with most strongly? Why?

3. Which statements were the most controversial? Were students able to defend their ideas?

For CNN video activities about debating gender differences, turn to page 199.

CHAPTER ⑩

IMMIGRATION: IS IT TIME TO SHUT THE DOOR?

PREVIEW

Discuss these questions with your classmates.

1. Have you ever lived in a different country? Would you ever move to a foreign country? Why or why not?

2. Does your native country have strict rules for immigration? Who is allowed in?

3. Have you ever lived in or near an immigrant neighborhood? If so, how did the native population feel about the immigrants?

PART I

Predict

A. Skim the readings and make predictions.

1. What part of the world is each reading about?
2. Which reading is from a newspaper?
3. Who is angry in each story?
4. Which article . . .

   a. uses quotations from government officials?

   b. talks about people who don't want to immigrate?

5. Predict the difficulty of each reading.

   a. Reading 1

   very easy   pretty easy   difficult   very difficult

   b. Reading 2

   very easy   pretty easy   difficult   very difficult

B. Write a question that you think each reading will answer.

Reading 1

_____

Reading 2

_____

Read It

Read the articles and look for the answers to your questions.

  READING 1

Native Sons (and Daughters) in Exile—
New Laws Force Danes to Sweden

COPENHAGEN—Most people think of Scandinavian countries as models of social awareness. As such, they have a long tradition of accepting immigrants from all over the world. But things are changing in Denmark. In fact, far from accepting foreigners, new immigration laws are even forcing native-born Danes into exile in neighboring Sweden.

Denmark's right-wing government was elected on an anti-immigration ticket and politicians are making good on their promises. The new immigration laws are meant to reduce the number of arranged and forced marriages among its Muslim ethnic minorities.

The laws, however, are also punishing indigenous or native-born Danes who marry foreigners from outside the European Union. For example, two months ago hospital worker Anders Koefod Hansen married a woman from Cameroon named Latay. She is facing expulsion from Denmark because the government suspects the couple of having a marriage of convenience. That is, they believe that Anders married her so that she could stay in Denmark.

Under the new rules, the government can expel a non-Danish spouse if they believe that person's ties to Denmark are not strong enough. "I love Anders and Anders loves me," says Latay. "I am ashamed of the government here. It is a shame that my husband is a Dane and yet he is having to leave Denmark."

The couple turned for help to Torben Bilken who runs Marriages Across Borders.

Young Dane pointing to Denmark

This organization helps couples move from Copenhagen to Malmo, Sweden, 30 kilometers away. Bilken explains that couples can live in Sweden for two years and then apply for Swedish citizenship. Ironically, once they legally become Swedes, they can move back to Denmark. In the meantime, most of them commute to work in Copenhagen.

Another clause of the new law bans immigrants under the age of 24 from marrying. This forces more couples into Swedish exile awaiting their twenty-fourth birthdays. According to Bertil Haader, the Integration Minister, this law is meant to prevent forced marriages among young people from Muslim backgrounds.

Although many people are calling the new laws absurd, the government shows no sign of changing its policies. Until the law is repealed, it seems that a large group of Danes will agree with Shakespeare's comment that there is "something rotten in the state of Denmark."

Adapted from "Denmark cracks down on migrant marriage," BBC News Online, with permission. Copyright © 2002 BBC.

How to Survive or
Illegal Immigration Made Easy?

MEXICO CITY, Jan. 5—Mexican officials are trying to explain the publication of a government comic-book guide for migrants. Critics say that it is actually an instruction booklet on how to illegally cross into the United States.

"We are a country that respects the law and we advise our people to respect the law," says Carlos de Icaza, Mexico's ambassador to the United States. He claims that the purpose of the new 32-page guide is to warn Mexicans not to illegally cross the U.S. border because hundreds die every year.

However, because the government knows that many Mexicans will risk the dangerous journey no matter what it mandates, the guide also explains how to make the trip more safely. For example, it tries to minimize the danger of drowning in the Rio Grande River by telling would-be migrants that, "heavy clothes get heavier when wet, making swimming or floating more difficult." Death from dehydration is also a major problem. To illegals crossing the Arizona desert, the guide advises, "Water with salt helps to retain the liquids in your body." The government is giving out 1.5 million copies of the comic book.

The booklet also gives advice on how to avoid being caught once you are in the United States. It warns immigrants to "avoid calling attention to yourself" and to stay away from loud parties because "neighbors could get mad and call the police." Immigrants are warned to leave immediately "if you go to a bar or a nightclub and a fight starts," because "you could be arrested, even if you didn't do anything."

Some U.S. lawmakers are furious about the booklet. They say that it is just a "how-to" guide for illegally entering the United States. Mexican officials said that the purpose of the guide has been misunderstood by critics. They note that the booklet clearly states that the only safe way to enter the United States is with a passport and visa. "Some are not interpreting the guide correctly," de Icaza says. He emphasizes that the guide also advises migrants not to use false documents, not to run away from border police or to throw rocks at them, and not to lie to a U.S. official.

Reading Comprehension

Check Your Predictions

1. Look back at questions 1–5 in the Predict section. How accurate were your predictions?

Prediction	Not Accurate	Accurate
1		
2		
3		
4a		
4b		
5a		
5b		

2. If you found the answers to your questions, what were they?

Reading 1

_____

Reading 2

_____

Check the Facts

READING 1

Write T for *true,* F for *false,* or NS for *not sure.*

_____ 1. Denmark is a Scandinavian country.

_____ 2. The new Danish laws were written by liberal legislators.

_____ 3. Most of Denmark's immigrants are Muslim.

_____ 4. Malmo, Sweden, is close to Copenhagen.

_____ 5. Anders Koefod Hansen will have to leave his job in Copenhagen.

_____ 6. Hansen and his wife will never be able to live in Denmark again.

_____ 7. According to Danish law, immigrants under 24 cannot marry at all.

_____ 8. Some Muslims are forced to marry although they do not want to.

READING 2

Check (✓) the questions you can answer after reading once. Then go back and look for the answers you are unsure of.

_____ 1. Who published the guide?

_____ 2. Was the guide written for legal or illegal immigrants?

_____ 3. What two major dangers do illegal immigrants face?

_____ 4. How can they avoid the police in the United States?

Analyze

Compare the two groups of immigrants discussed in Readings 1 and 2.

Which group . . .

    a. wants to immigrate?

    b. is immigrating legally?

    c. is immigrating to look for work?

    d. is getting help from their government?

    e. is getting help from a foreign government?

Vocabulary Work

Guess Meaning from Context

1. Look for these words in the readings.

Word	Reading	Meaning
exile	1	_____
ironically	1	_____
commute	1	_____
bans	1	_____
spouse	1	_____
journey	2	_____
minimize	2	_____
drowning	2	_____
dehydration	2	_____
retain	2	_____
documents	2	_____
border police	2	_____

2. A writer sometimes includes a definition or a synonym for a word or phrase that readers may not understand. What definition or synonym was given for these words and phrases?

marriage of convenience _____

indigenous _____

3. You can often guess the meaning of idioms just as you guess individual words. What do these idioms probably mean?

making good on _____

call attention to _____

4. Sometimes you can only guess the approximate meaning of a word. Look back at these words. Which meanings are possible? Which are very unlikely?

Reading 1

absurd: stupid   helpful   legal   European   good

Reading 2

furious: amused   confused   understanding   angry

Guess Meaning from Related Words

1. Sometimes we can recognize that words are related to words that we already know. What words are these related to?

neighboring _____

native-born _____

arranged _____

forced _____

booklet _____

2. Often, in a reading, you will find different forms of the same word. These words are occasionally related by suffixes. For example, you may find the verb *convict* and the noun *conviction*. Find other forms of these words in the readings.

Reading 1

Denmark _____

expel _____

immigrant _____

Reading 2

legal _____

immigrant _____

3. Work in pairs. Put the words from Exercise 2 in the correct columns. Compare your work with another pair when you are done.

Noun (person)	Noun (thing)	Verb	Adjective	Adverb

4. Look at the meanings of these prefixes. Then look for the words that use them in the readings and guess their meanings.

Prefix	Meaning	Word	Meaning
anti-	against	_____	_____
non-	not	_____	_____
mis-	wrong	_____	_____

Reading Skills

Understanding Cohesive Elements

Look at the <u>underlined</u> cohesive elements and read the sentences. Write the referents of these words and phrases on the line below.

1. <u>As such</u>, they have a long tradition of accepting immigrants from all over the world. _____

2. Denmark's right-wing government was elected on an anti-immigration ticket and politicians are making good on <u>their</u> promises.
_____

3. The new immigration laws are meant to reduce the number of arranged and forced marriages among <u>its</u> Muslim ethnic minorities.
_____

4. <u>That</u> is, they believe that Anders married her so that she could stay in Denmark. _____

5. Under the new rules, the government can expel a non-Danish spouse if they believe <u>that person's</u> ties to Denmark are not strong enough.
_____

6. <u>It</u> is a shame that my husband is a Dane and yet he is having to leave Denmark. _____

7. <u>This organization</u> helps couples move from Copenhagen to Malmo,

   _____

8. In the meantime, most of <u>them</u> commute to work in Copenhagen.

   _____

9. <u>This</u> forces more couples into Swedish exile awaiting their twenty-fourth birthdays. _____

10. Until the law is repealed <u>it</u> seems that a large group of Danes will agree with Shakespeare's comment that there is "something rotten in the state of Denmark." _____

Discussion

1. What is your opinion of the Danish government's new law? Give reasons for your answers.
2. Does the government of the United States have the right to be angry about the booklet? Why or why not?

PART II

This reading is more difficult than the articles in Part I. Read it for the main ideas. Do not worry if you cannot understand everything.

Read It

Read to find the answers to these questions.

1. What three things are governments trying to balance?
2. What are the two major groups of immigrants?
3. What are the concerns of native Europeans?
4. Are conservative groups for or against immigration? Why?
5. In what ways are immigrants mistreated?
6. Why are the governments worried about a labor shortage in the future?

READING

Immigration Confusion
Europe Struggles to Create a Balanced Immigration Policy

LONDON, England—Virtually every country in Europe is in an immigration mess. Governments are trying to balance the concerns of their citizens, their country's economic problems, and the humanitarian needs of immigrants. Native-born Europeans are worrying that their cultures and their economies are being harmed by immigrants. Meanwhile, the immigrants keep coming. Some come looking for asylum because of racial, religious, or political oppression in their native lands. Others are trying to escape grinding poverty or war at home.

With fifteen million people unemployed in the European Union (EU) alone, outsiders are often resented. Some people fear that asylum seekers are too expensive for the EU's social welfare systems. Others are worried that economic migrants may take their jobs. Still others worry about the weakening of traditional local cultures in places where there are large numbers of immigrants.

Right-wing parties in Austria, Denmark, and Belgium have successfully campaigned against immigration, using fears of the loss of national identity. Meanwhile, criminals are making money on the desperation of would-be immigrants. People-smuggling has become a highly organized and profitable business. Because smugglers care little for the people they are transporting, tragedies sometimes result. For example, in 2000, 58 illegal immigrants from China asphyxiated in a locked truck at the English port of Dover.

Even if they survive the trip, illegals are often mistreated in sweatshops, where they work for much less than normal wages in terrible conditions. Some of them spend decades paying back the transportation fees. Women and children are sometimes forced into sex slavery and prostitution.

To make matters even more confusing, there is another side to immigration. Many European countries have a shortage of skilled workers in areas like information technology. "We need immigration," declared German Chancellor Gerhard Schroeder recently. Barbara Roche, the UK's immigration minister, has made it easier for non-British students to stay. "In the past we have thought purely about immigration control," she said. "Now we need to think about immigration management."

High-tech workers are not the only ones who are needed. Some countries are short of cheap manual labor, too. In Spain, whose population is decreasing, North Africans work on the farms, while Poles and Romanians do construction work.

Retirement programs need immigrants, too. In most European nations, people are living longer and having fewer children. Governments will not be able to pay retirees without large-scale immigration. Jean-Pierre Chevenement, the former French interior minister, said Europe will need 50 million to 75 million immigrants during the next 50 years. In Italy there were eight workers to every retiree in the 1950s. There are fewer than four today and, without immigration, the figure will drop to 1.5 by 2050. Likewise, Germany will need three million immigrants a year to maintain the current ratio of workers to retirees.

Faced with these facts, it is not surprising that the European Union has said zero-immigration policies are unrealistic. One official states, "Our aim is to open as large a debate as possible on immigration and asylum."

Adapted from "Europe's tangle over immigration," by Robin Oakley, with permission. Copyright © 2001 CNN.

Vocabulary Work

Guess Words from Context

1. Do you need to understand all of these words to answer the prereading questions? Cross out (~~words~~) the words that you can ignore. <u>Underline</u> the words you know. (Circle) the words you need to guess.

mess	right-wing	slavery	manual
grinding	mistreated	high-tech	unrealistic
weakening	non-British	zero-immigration	asylum
asphyxiated	large-scale	economies	economic
skilled	native-born	resented	profitable
retirees	outsiders	would-be	shortage
balance	identity	prostitution	retirement
unemployed			

2. Try to use the following kinds of clues to help you understand the words from Exercise 1. Remember, it is often necessary to put several clues together in order to make a good guess. Write the words below the clue or clues that you used.

It looks like a word I know and/or I understood the prefix or suffix.

_____

I used my knowledge of immigration.

_____

I used my knowledge of politics and economics.

_____

I used logic.

_____

The writer gave a definition or explanation.

_____

Reading Skills

Understanding Organization

Complete the diagram about the reading. Look for the main idea and supporting details.

_____ (main idea)

Arguments in Favor of Immigration

_____   _____

economic burden   _____

_____   _____

_____   _____

_____   _____

Idea Exchange

Think about Your Ideas

1. People immigrate for many different reasons. Look at the list of reasons. Add any others that you can think of.

Reasons people immigrate	A	B
political freedom		
religious tolerance		
economic opportunity		
war		
health		
family reunification		
other reasons:		

2. a. In column A above, number the reasons in order of importance or _legitimacy._ For example, if you think the most valid reason for immigrating is political freedom, mark it as number 1.

   b. In column B, number the reasons in the order of the number of people who come for that reason. For example, if you think most people come to find religious tolerance, mark it as number 1.

3. Why do countries like or need immigrants? List positive aspects of immigration from the point of view of the receiving country.

_____

_____

_____

_____

4. Why do countries oppose immigration? List negative aspects of immigration from the point of view of the receiving country.

_____

_____

_____

_____

Talk about Your Ideas

Discuss these questions with your classmates.

1. Some people in countries that receive many immigrants believe that there need to be stricter immigration policies. How far should a country go to protect its identity? its native culture? How open should a society be to people from other parts of the world?

2. Some people see those who emigrate from their native country as *traitors*. Do you agree? Why or why not?

3. Would you ever immigrate to another country? Why or why not?

For CNN video activities about immigration in middle America, turn to page 200.

CHAPTER 11

BUSINESS:
GLOBALIZATION OR CULTURAL IMPERIALISM?

a.

b.

c.

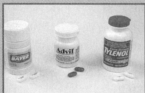
d.

e.

f.

g.

h.

i.

j.

PREVIEW

1. Do you recognize the company brand logos and mottos above? What products are the companies most famous for? Match the words below with the logos above.

a. _____ sneakers or running shoes

b. _____ TV station

c. _____ blue jeans

d. _____ hamburgers

e. _____ cars

f. _____ medicine for pain

g. _____ soda

h. _____ underwear

i. _____ chocolate

j. _____ women's clothing

2. Do you buy products from these companies? Are there any of these companies you <u>don't</u> buy from? Why?

PART I

Predict

A. Skim the readings and make predictions.

1. Which reading . . .
   a. gives opinions?
   b. defends the United States?
   c. was not written by an American?
   d. discusses a number of different countries?

2. Predict the difficulty of each reading.
   a. Reading 1

      very easy   pretty easy   difficult   very difficult
   b. Reading 2

      very easy   pretty easy   difficult   very difficult

B. Write a question that you think each reading will answer.

Reading 1

_____

Reading 2

_____

Read It

Read the articles and look for the answers to your questions.

 READING 1

English: Can Anyone Stop It? Should They Try?

English is spoken by approximately two billion people around the world, and this number is growing by leaps and bounds. Many people are not happy about this. They deplore the need to learn English. According to these people, learning English is bad enough, but what is worse is the hybridization of English and their native language. By a language hybrid, I mean a combination of two different languages.

The most famous hybrid is probably Spanglish—a combination of Spanish and English commonly used in Hispanic communities in the United States. Spanglish is rapidly moving from a cultural oddity to a serious language. In 2004, the first academic conference on Spanglish was held at Amherst College in Massachusetts. Attendees heard talks on Spanglish linguistics, Spanglish media, Spanglish culture, and Spanglish arts. The conference was organized by Professor Ilan Stavans, who is writing the first Spanglish-English dictionary. When asked if he considered Spanglish the result of cultural imperialism, he said, "I'd describe it more as cultural irrigation than cultural imperialism. The U.S. is a laboratory of languages which are fertilizing each other," says Stavans. "Language has its own ways and Spanglish is a movement which is happening and happening globally. It's too free to be pinned down and it's impossible to legislate its usage."

Meanwhile, in Europe, traditionalists are trying to hold back the flood of English. Both Spain and France have academies that were created hundreds of years ago to protect the purity of the Spanish and French languages. In Spain, they are losing the battle. The French, always cautious about outside cultural influences, are having greater success.

In Germany, where English, or *Denglish (Deutsch + English)*, is often used in advertisements, there is a movement to go back to the language of Goethe. Not long ago, Lufthansa changed its slogan from "There's No Better Way to Fly," in English, to the German "Alles für diesen Moment," or "Everything for This Moment." Similarly, German McDonald's changed its slogan from "Every time a good time" to "Ich liebe es," which translates to "I love it." Unfortunately, for German traditionalists, there has also been some movement in the other direction. A German Burger King recently changed its slogan to the English "Feel the Fire."

All over the world there are people who are worried about losing their native languages and others who feel that languages have always intermixed and that this trend is no different. At any rate, what authority does any nation have to control the changes in its language and to guard against words from other languages?

READING 2

American Music Tops the Charts in England

When this week's singles chart is announced tomorrow, the top five are expected to be from across the Atlantic. The likely success of Eminem, Destiny's Child, Christina Aguilera, Usher, and Britney Spears is to many a welcome "shot in the arm"—good for the sale of singles. But some people are worried.

Some of our countrymen fondly recall forty years ago when the Beatles led the British invasion of the American music scene. Now the situation is reversed. Some say that the dominance of a few major U.S. record company labels is leading to a homogenous, Americanized pop culture.

Martin Mills, head of an independent label, said, "I hate to use words like 'cultural imperialism' but American cultural hegemony is the corporate music order of the day." Alison Wenham, the chief executive of the Association of Independent Music (AIM) agrees. She says that mergers between record companies has to stop. "It's about defending cultural diversity, consumer choice, and the ability for artists to make a living. These big, multinationals are less interested in signing, nurturing, and developing local talent. As a result, we end up in a situation where the top of the charts is all internationally marketable, American artists."

For their part, spokesmen from the major record companies disagree. "This year has been one of our best for breaking new British acts," said Adam White, communications vice-president at Universal Music International. Moreover, he points out that the top five singles sellers of the year were all British. And the news for albums is even better. Sixteen of this week's top 20 are British.

Furthermore, it looks like British bands are doing better in the United States as well. Steve Redmond of the British Phonographic Industry compares the situation today with the recent past. "A couple of years ago, U.K. [British] music looked in pretty poor health, with not a single act in the American top 100 for the first time in decades. But now you've got bands like Franz Ferdinand, The Darkness, and Snow Patrol who have all had good years in the States."

Wenham is not impressed. She points out that 25 years ago, British bands had 30 percent of the U.S. market. Today it is 1.7 percent. Still, the large corporations say that it's all just sour grapes. If consumers choose to buy more Britney Spears records than Jamelia, that's their right.

What may be viewed as one country's cultural imperialism can also be looked at as a country's proud export. Robbie Williams, a U.K. megastar, currently has the best selling album in Europe and tops the album charts in Germany, Spain, Portugal, Holland, and Switzerland. British musicians such as Depeche Mode, Mark Knopler, Phil Collins, Joss Stone, the Rolling Stones, Queen, Duran Duran, Ronan Keating, and Placebo have hit albums in Europe.

No one minds that British artists are popular in the European Union. So how can we complain when U.S. artists are a success in the U.K.?

Reading Comprehension

Check Your Predictions

1. Look back at questions 1 and 2 in the Predict section. How accurate were your predictions?

Prediction	Not Accurate	Accurate
1a		
1b		
1c		
1d		
2a		
2b		

2. If you found the answers to your questions, what were they?

Reading 1

_____

Reading 2

_____

Check the Facts

READING 1

Write T for *true,* F for *false,* or NS for *not sure.*

_____ 1. Spanglish is a hybrid language.

_____ 2. Some people believe that Spanglish is a serious language.

_____ 3. Spanglish is spoken in Mexico.

_____ 4. The French do not like to adopt aspects of other cultures.

_____ 5. Denglish is a mixture of Dutch and English.

_____ 6. Some companies in Germany use English slogans.

_____ 7. English is becoming less popular in German advertising.

_____ 8. Some people believe that soon the whole world will be speaking English.

READING 2

Write T for *true,* **F for** *false,* **or NS for** *not sure.*

_____ 1. British music used to be much more popular in the United States than it is today.

_____ 2. American music isn't very popular in Britain.

_____ 3. There are fewer record companies than there used to be.

_____ 4. Most large record companies are European.

_____ 5. Albums by British musicians sell better in Britain than singles by British musicians.

_____ 6. Several British bands are very popular in the European Union.

_____ 7. The writer is British.

Analyze

1. Does the writer of Reading 1 believe that language academies are effective?

2. Does the writer of Reading 2 probably agree with . . .

   Martin Mills?

   Alison Wenham?

   Adam White?

   Steve Redmond?

3. Do the writers of Reading 1 and Reading 2 probably agree with each other?

Vocabulary Work

Guess Meaning from Context

1. Look for these words in the readings. Decide if they are necessary to understanding the authors' main ideas. Use the following types of clues to guess the meaning of the important words:

   • knowledge of language

   • knowledge of advertising

   • knowledge of the music industry

   • logic

   • examples in the reading

   • definitions or synonyms in the reading

Word	Reading	Meaning
deplore	1	_____
slogan	1	_____
key	1	_____
aspect	1	_____
phenomenon	1	_____
top	2	_____
singles	2	_____
chart	2	_____
fondly	2	_____
reversed	2	_____
homogeneous	2	_____
hegemony	2	_____
mergers	2	_____
nurturing	2	_____
album	2	_____
export	2	_____

2. The readings contain a number of idiomatic phrases. Guess their meanings.

READING 1

leaps and bounds _____

pinned down _____

losing the battle _____

READING 2

a shot in the arm _____

sour grapes _____

3. Reading 1 contains a German cultural reference. Who or what was Goethe?

4. Sometimes writers use familiar words in a *metaphorical* way. For example, these three words usually refer to farming. What do they mean in the context of Reading 1?

hybrid _____

irrigation _____

fertilizing _____

Guess Meaning from Related Words

1. Another very important strategy is to relate new words to words that you already know. Underline the common words in these compound words. Try to guess the meaning.

Word	Reading	Meaning
intermixed	1	_____
recall	2	_____

2. Find other forms of these words in the readings.

odd   _____

attend   _____

pure   _____

dominate   _____

market   _____

3. Work in pairs. Put the words from Exercises 1 and 2 in the correct columns. Compare your work with another pair when you are done.

Noun (person)	Noun (thing)	Verb	Adjective	Adverb

4. Look at the meanings of these prefixes. Then look for the words in the readings that use them and guess their meanings.

Prefix	Meaning	Word	Meaning
multi-	many	_____	_____
mega-	great, large	_____	_____

Reading Skills

Understanding Transition Words and Phrases

Look for the following transition words and phrases in the readings. Explain what ideas they connect.

Transition Word or Phrase	Function	Reading
meanwhile	time	1
at any rate	concession	1
as a result	result	2
for their part	in addition	2
moreover	in addition	2
still	exception	2

Discussion

1. How is English used in your country? Has a hybrid language developed? How do people feel about the use of English?

2. Is Western music popular in your country? If so, is most of it American, European, or a combination?

PART II

This reading is more difficult than the articles in Part I. Read it for the main ideas. Do not worry if you cannot understand everything.

Read It

Read to find the answers to these questions.

1. How do people outside the United States feel about American culture?

2. What country in Europe is most against American cultural imperialism?

3. Does the writer feel that this country has the right to be upset? Why or why not?

4. Where are Americans worried about cultural imperialism?

5. What is the "law of cultural dominance"?

6. What other reasons do some people give for domination of one culture?

7. Who are the Amish? Where do they live? How do they live?

8. Does the author believe that cultural imperialism is inevitable and evil?

Adapted from **The Myth of Cultural Imperialism**
by Robert K. Rauth, Jr.

What do Mickey Mouse, Ronald McDonald, and Superman have in common? They are all easily identified and powerful symbols of what some people call American "cultural imperialism." Most Americans would be surprised that these beloved cultural icons are often unwelcome by many overseas.

The cries of cultural imperialism are a relatively recent phenomenon. With the shrinking of Western colonial empires in Asia, Africa, and South America, nationalists in the newly independent countries often became outraged over the staying power of <u>colonial cultures</u>. These nationalists named the presence and domination of Western culture as "<u>cultural imperialism</u>." Paul Harrison in his book, *Inside the Third World*, described it this way, "And so there grew up, alongside political and economic imperialism, that more insidious form of control—cultural imperialism. It conquered not just the bodies, but the souls of its victims."

In time, the strength and attraction of Western popular culture became even more dominated by that of the United States. This development allowed the accusations of cultural imperialism to become just as common in European intellectual circles as in the developing "Third World." In other words, not only the leftists feared cultural domination. Both left and right worked together to oppose American influence in their countries.

Because the French have traditionally been very proud of their culture, the emergence of American popular culture has been an especially bitter pill for them to swallow. The fear of encroaching Americana has often been on the mind of France's Minister of Culture, Jack Lang. Shortly after the Socialist Party's election in the 1980's, Lang called "for a real crusade against . . . this financial and intellectual imperialism that no longer grabs territory . . . but grabs consciousness, ways of thinking, ways of living." [. . .]

Uniting Against "Pollution"

The cries against cultural imperialism, however, are not restricted to the world's leftists. In fact, the fear of American cultural imperialism has created a powerful response from the world's elite, regardless of their political position. The left and right have often joined forces against the American "pollution" of their native culture. While leftists are disgusted by the strength and attraction of a base, capitalistic culture—one that emphasizes money, lust, and power—conservatives also lament the democratization of their "civilization." [. . .]

Despite the popularity of American food, music, fashion, and movies among the French middle class, the attacks on America's pop culture by French intellectuals have been particularly cutting. A popular magazine *Le Nouvel Observateur* featured a cover with Mickey Mouse

high above the Eiffel Tower. The headline read: "Is this Mouse Dangerous?" In the accompanying article, one writer likened Disneyland to a "degenerate utopia." One of the leading French newspapers, *Le Matin,* warned that the European Disneyland will "deform generations of French children." [. . .]

Of course, for Europe—particularly France—to make any complaint about American cultural imperialism is pure hypocrisy. The French had no misgivings about cultural imperialism when their culture was dominant. No one complained about sending priests and bureaucrats to colonize West Africa. As David Lamb, author of *The Africans,* writes: "[in French West Africa, France] remains the paramount economic and cultural force. . . . Unlike other colonial powers, France governed through a policy of assimilation or, as some have called it, cultural imperialsim."

Which Culture Dominates?

America itself is not immune to the fear of cultural imperialism. Those who dislike the spread of American culture will be surprised to learn that Americans themselves also fear cultural imperialism. Indeed, those who live in the enormous center of the United States, often complain that the "alien cultures" of New York and Los Angeles are much too influential. Americans living between Los Angeles and New York resent the cultural products of these two "foreign capitals." More serious is the risk posed by what anthropologists term "the law of cultural dominance." This theory states that whichever culture is technologically superior will eventually dominate its inferiors. [. . .]

At the moment, however, American culture is best symbolized by cultural technology. Because of the eagerness of many countries to adopt new technologies, there are few complaints about cultural imperialism when it comes to sharing current technological advances. Most cultures are welcoming of American technological advances. But vaccines, telephones, and airplanes are as symbolic of America as Mickey Mouse and Ronald McDonald. Once American technology is introduced—even though technology is generally considered non-imperialistic—a closer mirroring of the United States is likely to follow. For example, once cars become important to a society, road systems and cities designed to accommodate the vehicles will result. Thus, a more American-looking city is created. As a faster lifestyle comes about, fast-food restaurants such as McDonald's and Kentucky Fried Chicken become more acceptable and necessary.

This trend is especially well demonstrated by the success that these two chains have had in the rapidly developing Asian market. For example, McDonald's highest sales per store have been recorded in Taiwan while Kentucky Fried Chicken's most successful franchise is found in Malaysia. The chains admit that their success has been greatly dependent on these countries' economic development and the rapid growth of their cities. [. . .]

Cultural Imperialism in Miami

One of the best environments in which to examine cultural imperialism lies not in Western Europe or in developing countries but in Miami, Florida. Anglos and Blacks in that city frequently object to Hispanic cultural imperialism. As one bumper sticker states: "Will the Last American to Leave Miami Please Bring the Flag?" With over 40 per cent of the city's population Hispanic, non-Hispanics often feel like strangers in their own country. They point to Miami's two Spanish-language newspapers, two television stations, six radio stations,

(Continued on next page)

and the political domination of Hispanics. Anglos and Blacks are especially incensed that Miami residents increasingly need to learn two languages—an obstacle that has particularly hampered employment opportunities. For instance, a recent discrimination complaint was filed by two Miami women who were refused jobs as cleaning women in a downtown office building because they couldn't speak Spanish. [. . .]

What all of this means is that the United States is as influenced by outside cultures as other countries are influenced by the U.S. For example, Americans do not resent, but enjoy Jamaican reggae, Chinese restaurants, and British comedy. Looking at the difficulties in Miami, the mixing of cultures is not always easy. But those who argue against America's cultural imperialism should realize that closing a society is no solution to preventing outside influences. The most insular societies have the least to offer culturally to the masses. Despite its previous dedication to the world's working classes, it is ironic that the former Soviet Union's most vital cultural export—ballet—has not been appreciated by the proletariat or the working class, but by the wealthy and highly educated: the world's elite. [. . .]

Most of us would regret the world's becoming a standardized and uniform culture. After all, finding a McDonald's in Katmandu, Nepal, would make that town a little less exotic and special. But who are we to tell the Nepalese that they shouldn't have a McDonald's? Let their wallets decide.

This adaptation of "The Myth of Cultural Imperialism" is reprinted by permission of Leslie Pietrzyk, for the estate of Robert K. Rauth, Jr. The complete essay is available at www.fee.org and was originally published in The Freeman: Ideas on Liberty. Copyright © 1988

Vocabulary Work

Guess Meaning from Context

1. Do you need to understand all of these words to answer the prereading questions? Cross out (~~word~~) the words that you can ignore. <u>Underline</u> the words you know. (Circle) the words you need to guess.

beloved	insidious	democratization
leftists	disgusted	assimilation
unlike	paramount	deform
hypocrisy	elite	influential
technologically	encroaching	insular
overseas	grab	

2. Try to use the following kinds of clues to help you understand the words. Remember, it is often necessary to put several clues together in order to make a good guess. Write the word under the clue you used to guess its meaning.

It looks like a word I know and/or I understood the prefix or suffix.

_____

I used my knowledge of American culture.

_____

I used my knowledge of other cultures.

_____

I used my knowledge of economics.

_____

I used logic.

_____

The writer gave a definition or explanation.

_____

The writer gave an example.

_____

Reading Skills

Evaluating Different Types of Supporting Details

*Look back at the examples of different types of supporting details given in Chapter 3, page 41. There is another type of supporting detail that writers use when they are defending an idea—***logical argument.**

> Some experts say that fat is unhealthy. They claim that those who eat fatty foods such as cream, butter, and bacon are at much greater risk for heart attacks. If this were true, then the French—whose diet is very high in fat—should be dying from heart attacks at an amazing rate. However, statistics show that the French have many fewer heart attacks than Americans.

Once you identify the logical argument, you need to evaluate it. Reread the paragraph above. Is the writer's conclusion adequately supported? Why or why not?

Look back at the reading. First, identify the main ideas. Next, identify the type of supporting detail used for each one. Finally, decide if the detail gives adequate support to the main idea.

Idea Exchange

Think about Your Ideas

1. Look at the list on the next page. How often do you use or buy products from these places in the chart?

←   1   2   3   4   5 →

almost always   usually   sometimes   rarely   never

Product	Locally made	Foreign, but not American	American
music			
movies			
food			
television			
clothing			
electronics			
cars			
large appliances			

2. If you buy imported products rather than locally made products, why do you do it? Think of product or brand examples for each one of the following reasons:

   a. Imports are less expensive.

   b. Imports are better.

   c. Imports are more well-known.

   d. Imports are more stylish or up-to-date.

   e. It is impossible to find a locally made product.

   f. Other _____

3. When is English used in your culture? Check (✓) the reasons that are true.

   _____ Only as a foreign language—for reading academic journals or technical material.

   _____ Educated people often use English words or expressions in their conversation.

   _____ Most people use a few English words or expressions in their conversations.

   _____ Advertisements use English words or expressions.

   _____ Most everyone is almost bilingual in English and our native language.

_____ Some people use a hybrid of English and our native language in informal conversations.

_____ Most young people have learned some English through songs and music.

Talk About Your Ideas

1. Should people always try to buy domestic products? Why or why not?

2. Is English an important means of communication in your culture? Why or why not?

For CNN video activities about globalization and cultural imperialism, turn to page 201.

CHAPTER 12

Sex Education:
How much do we need to know?

PREVIEW

Which statements do you most agree with? Which ones do you most disagree with?

1. Sex is a natural part of human behavior and people should feel free to talk about it openly.

2. Sex is a private matter that should not be discussed outside the home.

3. The more young people learn about sex in the classroom, the more likely they are to make good choices in their private lives.

4. Schools should be working against the bad sexual messages young people hear and see in music, in movies, and on television.

5. No type of sexual behavior between consenting adults is bad.

6. Discussing sex leads to immoral behavior.

PART I

Predict

A. Skim the readings and make predictions.

1. Which reading . . .

    a. describes sex education programs?

    b. compares two different sex education programs?

    c. includes statistics?

    d. calls on people to do something?

2. Predict the difficulty of each reading.

    a. Reading 1

    very easy   pretty easy   difficult   very difficult

    b. Reading 2

    very easy   pretty easy   difficult   very difficult

B. Write a question that you think each reading will answer.

Reading 1: _____

Reading 2: _____

Read It

Read the articles and answer your questions.

 READING 1

What Is Sex Education?

Sex education, which is sometimes called *sexuality education* or *sex and relationships education*, is the process of acquiring information and forming attitudes and beliefs about sex, sexual identity, relationships, and intimacy. Sex education is not meant to replace the role of parents. It does not teach children what is morally correct. Sex education simply gives young people information so that they can make informed choices about their behavior. It also teaches them skills so that they feel confident and competent about acting on these choices. In short, sex education helps young people protect themselves against abuse, exploitation, unintended pregnancies, and sexually transmitted diseases such as syphilis and HIV-AIDS.

(Continued on next page)

Developing Life Skills

The kinds of skills young people develop as part of sex education are similar to more general life skills. For example, they are taught to communicate effectively. This includes listening, negotiating, identifying reliable sources of help and advice, and then asking for help and advice. Other important skills include being able to recognize and resist pressure or coercion from others, and dealing with prejudice. Effective sex education also teaches young people to differentiate between accurate and inaccurate information and gives them the tools to discuss perspectives on sex and sexuality, including different cultural attitudes and sensitive issues like sexual preference, abortion, and contraception.

Forming Attitudes and Beliefs

In today's society, young people see and hear a wide range of attitudes and beliefs about sex and sexuality. These attitudes are often contradictory and confusing. For example, some health messages emphasize the risks and dangers associated with sexual activity while television programs, advertisements, music, and movies often imply that being sexually active makes a person more attractive and mature. Young people are very interested in the moral and cultural basis of sex and sexuality. They often welcome opportunities to talk about issues where people have strong views, such as abortion, sex before marriage, lesbian and gay issues, and contraception and birth control. It is important to remember that talking in a balanced way about differences in opinion does not promote one set of views over another. Part of exploring and understanding cultural, religious, and moral views is finding out that you can agree to disagree.

Of course, sex education teachers have their own beliefs about sex and sexuality, but they should not allow these beliefs to influence their teaching in a negative way. For example, even if a person believes that young people should not have sex until they are married, they still must teach about safe sex and contraception. Rather than trying to stop young people from having sex, effective sex education enables young people to choose whether or not to have a sexual relationship while taking into account the potential risks of any sexual activity.

An effective sex education program

- has a focus on reducing specific risky behaviors;
- has a sound scientific basis;
- has a clear message about sexual behavior and risk reduction;
- provides accurate information about the risks associated with sexual activity, contraception and birth control, and methods of avoiding or postponing intercourse;
- provides opportunities to practice communication, negotiation, and assertion skills;
- uses approaches to teaching and learning that are appropriate to young people's age, experience, and cultural background.

Reprinted from "Sex Education That Works" with permission. Copyright © 2005 AVERT (www.avert.org)

Washington Needs a Reality Check

"People should only have sex within a mutually faithful monogamous marriage." Different people will disagree about the validity of this statement, but few would say that it describes the experiences of the majority of American teenagers. Despite reality, the federal government says that all sex education programs must be based on this unrealistic principle.

Current Status

The United States has the highest rates of teenage pregnancies and cases of sexually transmitted diseases (STDs) of any developed nation. Furthermore, every year approximately 10,000 people under the age of 22 contract HIV-AIDS. The vast majority of these new cases are the result of sexual activity. Experts say that restriction to sex education, contraception, and condoms are the cause. They compare the United States with Europe, where teens can easily obtain contraceptives. While in European countries teenagers are as sexually active as Americans, they have less than half of the rate of teen pregnancies.

In 2004, National Public Radio, the Kaiser Family Foundation, and Harvard's Kennedy School of Government conducted a survey about American attitudes toward sex education. Thirty-six percent of Americans believe that schools should teach that abstinence is best, but that they should also teach teenagers about contraception. These programs are usually called *abstinence plus.* Only 15 percent of those polled believed that sex education should be *abstinence only.* This type of program only gives teenagers information about why they should not have sex before marriage. Unfortunately, according to current U.S. law, abstinence-plus programs receive no money from Washington. The federal government will only fund abstinence-only programs.

The following table compares the two types of sex education programs:

Abstinence-Plus Education	Abstinence-Only Education
• Promotes abstinence from sex. • Acknowledges that many teenagers will become sexually active. • Teaches about contraception and condoms. • Include discussions about abortion, sexually transmitted diseases (STDs), and HIV/AIDS.	• Promotes abstinence from sex. • Does not acknowledge that many teenagers will become sexually active. • Does not teach about contraception and condoms. • Avoids discussions of abortion. • Says that STDs and HIV/AIDS are reasons to remain abstinent.

(Continued on next page)

A 2002 report by AIDS Research Institute at the University of California, San Francisco, concludes:

> The growing prominence of the abstinence-only approach will likely have serious unintended consequences by denying young people access to the information they need to protect themselves. And abstinence-only programs risk alienating the young people at highest risk . . . by promoting a "one size fits all" vision of adolescence that matches the true experiences of only a minority of youth.

It's time for lawmakers to admit that the law flies in the face of reality. As much as we might not like it, many of our young people are having sex. If there is any sin here, it is not giving them the information that they need to protect themselves.

Reading Comprehension

Check Your Predictions

1. Look back at questions 1 and 2 in the Predict section. How accurate were your predictions?

Prediction	Not Accurate	Accurate
1a		
1b		
1c		
1d		
2a		
2b		

2. If you found the answers to your questions, what were they?

Reading 1

_____

Reading 2

_____

Check the Facts

READING 1

1. Circle the topics the author says that sex education programs cover.

   abortion   birth control   morality

   STDs   history   sex techniques

   pornography   sexual identity   avoiding risks

2. According to the writer, what skills does a good sex education program teach?

   _____ negotiation

   _____ exploitation

   _____ toleration

   _____ finding information

3. Why does the writer say that young people get contradictory messages about sex?

READING 2

Check (✓) the questions you can answer after reading once. Then go back and look for the answers that you are unsure of.

_____ 1. What two programs does the article compare?

_____ 2. Which program does the writer think is best?

_____ 3. Which program does the federal government support?

_____ 4. How do American and European teenage pregnancy rates compare?

_____ 5. What does the writer believe the reason for this is?

_____ 6. What percentage of Americans believe that abstinence is best?

_____ 7. Does the AIDS Research Institute agree with the writer? Why or why not?

_____ 8. What does the writer think is a "sin"?

Analyze

Compare the description of abstinence-only programs with the bulleted list at the end of Reading 1. Would the writer of Reading 1 believe that abstinence-only was a good program? Why or why not?

Vocabulary Work

Guess Meaning from Context

1. Look for these words in the readings. Decide if they are necessary
   to understand in the reading. Use these types of clues to guess their
   meanings.

   • knowledge of education

   • knowledge of sex

   • logic

   • examples in the reading

   • definitions or synonyms in the reading

Word	Reading	Meaning
acquire	1	_____
intimacy	1	_____
negotiating	1	_____
reliable	1	_____
coercion	1	_____
abortion	1	_____
imply	1	_____
mature	1	_____
lesbian and gay	1	_____
promote	1	_____
intercourse	1	_____
principle	2	_____
STDs	2	_____
condoms	2	_____
abstinence	2	_____
prominence	2	_____
sin	2	_____

2. What do these idioms from Reading 2 mean?

   one size fits all _____

   flies in the face of reality _____

3. What does *plus* mean in the phrase *abstinence plus*?

   _____

Guess Meaning from Related Words

1. Find other forms of these words in the readings.

Reading 1

inform _____   exploit _____   different _____

sex _____   able _____   reduce _____

Reading 2

monogamy _____   abstain _____   alienate _____

2. Work in pairs. Put the words from Exercises 1 and 2 in the correct columns. Compare your work with another pair when you are done.

Noun (person)	Noun (thing)	Verb	Adjective	Adverb

3. Look at the meanings of these prefixes. Then look for the words that use them in the readings and guess their meanings.

Prefix	Meaning	Word	Meaning
un-	not	_____	_____
		_____	_____
		_____	_____
in-	in, into, not	_____	_____
		_____	_____
		_____	_____
		_____	_____
inter-	between	_____	_____
contra-	against	_____	_____
		_____	_____
		_____	_____

Reading Skills

Understanding Transition Words

Transition words and phrases *show connections between ideas in a reading. You are probably familiar with some of the most common transitional phrases and connectors:*

> but   however   although   then   next

In more advanced reading, there are a number of less common but important transition words and phrases.

Look for the following words and phrases in the readings. Identify the ideas that they connect.

Reading	Transition Word or Phrase	Function
Reading 1	of course	emphasizes an idea
Reading 1	in short	restates an idea
Reading 2	despite	gives a contrast or comparison
Reading 2	as much as	gives a contrast or comparison
Reading 2	while	gives a contrast or comparison
Reading 2	furthermore	adds information

Discussion

1. Do you think that schools should offer sex education programs? Why or why not?

2. Would you prefer an abstinence-only or an abstinence-plus program? Why?

PART II

This reading is more difficult than the articles in Part I. Read it for the main ideas. Do not worry if you cannot understand everything.

Read It

Read to find the answers to these questions.

1. How did people feel about sex when Kinsey was growing up?
2. What was Kinsey's educational background?
3. How did he begin teaching sex education?
4. How did he conduct his research?
5. Why were people upset when he published his research on men?
6. How did they feel when he published his research on women?
7. What happened as a result?
8. How do people feel about him today?

 READING

Alfred Kinsey— The Man Who Pulled Back the Covers

The man who became known as the first and greatest reporter of America's sexual experiences was born in Hoboken, New Jersey, on June 23, 1894. Alfred Kinsey grew up in a world where sex education was almost unheard of. Sex was still a "dirty secret." Married people did it—but only husbands enjoyed it. Single people didn't do it at all. If homosexuals did it, they went to jail. But, most importantly, no matter if you did it or not, you didn't talk about it.

Providing Information

Trained as a biologist, Kinsey taught at Indiana University. He first taught about insects. Then he became interested in sex education. He insisted that sex education should go beyond biology and teach children

(Continued on next page)

healthy attitudes about sex. He and his wife, Clara, began by informally advising university students about sex. Undergraduates often spent long afternoons at the Kinseys' house drinking tea and talking about sex. Upset at how little young people knew about sex, in 1938, Kinsey asked for permission to offer a "marriage course." He got permission to teach the course but only to seniors and married students.

Instantly Popular Course

In the course, Kinsey argued that sex was the glue that held human societies together. He attacked the role of religious institutions in regulating sexual conduct. Kinsey was extremely candid, discussing the most intimate details of sexual behavior without embarrassment or euphemisms, and using drawings showing the details of sexual intercourse. While he based the course on science, he used it to argue strongly for the sexual liberation of males and females alike.

The course was an immediate hit. Kinsey then decided that he should use his students to begin a study of human sexuality. He began asking students to complete a questionnaire on their sexual histories. Kinsey soon moved from questionnaires to interviews because he believed that he would get more truthful and complete answers. The interviews lasted several hours and consisted of between 300 and 521 questions. To persuade people to share their deepest secrets, Kinsey promised his volunteers total confidentiality. He even hired a cryptographer to develop a code for recording the results of each interview so that respondents were completely anonymous. This code was known only to Kinsey and his assistants, and it was never written down.

Sensational Findings

In 1948, Kinsey published part of the results of his work entitled *Sexual Behavior in the Human Male.* The book's contents were startling to many. Kinsey's research showed that the sex lives of many men did not correspond to the American myth that men only had sex with their wives. The book went right to the top of the best-seller lists, but there were many critics. Some felt human sexuality was not a suitable topic for public discussion; others disagreed with Kinsey's research methods. Some stated that sexuality could not be studied without also talking about morality.

(Continued on next page)

The reaction to the report on men was mild compared to the firestorm that started when he published his research on females in 1953. According to Kinsey's statistics, more than 50 percent of American women had had premarital sex and 26 percent had had extramarital affairs. Kinsey used these numbers to argue that women were no less sexual than men and had as much right to expect sexual satisfaction. He also claimed that a satisfying sex life was essential to a happy marriage. Perhaps his most controversial conclusion was that women who had had sex before marriage were more likely to have happy, sexually satisfying marriages than those who had not.

Although some people were grateful to Kinsey, many were upset and angry. There were a lot who argued that the statistics couldn't be accurate because "good" women would not have taken part in such activities, and if they had, they would not have told Dr. Kinsey. Prominent religious leaders such as the Reverend Billy Graham condemned the work. He declared that Dr. Kinsey "certainly could not have interviewed any of the millions of born-again Christian women in this country who put the highest price on virtue, decency, and modesty."

In the end, the public outcry was too much for the politicians and Kinsey lost government financial support for his research. He died on August 25, 1956, disappointed that he had not persuaded the world that sex was good and that tolerance of many different sexual behaviors was right. Decades after his death, Kinsey's work is still controversial. While some still criticize his methodology, no one can deny that he is in a large part responsible for the academic freedom researchers now have to discuss topics that were once taboo.

Vocabulary Work

Guess Words from Context

1. Do you need to understand all of these words to answer the prereading questions? Cross out the words (~~word~~) that you can ignore. <u>Underline</u> the words you know. (Circle) the words you need to guess.

unheard of	dirty secret	informally	undergraduates
glue	institutions	embarrassment	euphemisms
intercourse	alike	questionnaire	deepest
cryptographer	code	anonymous	startling
critics	suitable	morality	firestorm
premarital	extramarital	satisfying	prominent
modesty	outcry	tolerance	decades
methodology	taboo		

2. Try to use the following kinds of clues to help you understand the words in Exercise 1. Remember, it is often necessary to put several clues together in order to make a good guess. Write the words under the clue you used to understand each one.

It looks like a word I know and/or I understood the prefix or suffix.

_____

I used my knowledge of society in the 1940s and 1950s.

_____

I used my knowledge of sex education.

_____

I used logic.

_____

The writer gave a definition or explanation.

_____

The writer gave an example.

_____

Reading Skills

Understanding Introductory Phrases

Introductory phrases *give information about the subject or verb and come before the main sentence or clause. The phrase is separated from the subject by a comma.*

Rewrite the following sentences in more common word order.

1. Trained as a biologist, Kinsey taught at Indiana University.

_____

_____

2. Upset at how little young people knew about sex, in 1938, Kinsey asked for permission to offer a "marriage course."

_____

_____

3. To persuade people to share their deepest secrets, Kinsey promised his volunteers total confidentiality.

_____

_____

4. Decades after his death, Kinsey's work is still controversial.

_____

_____

Idea Exchange

Think about Your Ideas

1. **Where** should students learn about these topics—if you think they should learn about them at all? Are there any others that you would add?

Topic	In school	At home	From friends	From popular culture	They shouldn't learn this.
human reproduction					
contraception					
abortion					
sexually transmitted diseases					
homosexuality					
safe sex					
sexual morality					
other topic					

2. How would you feel if you were asked to participate in a confidential study of human sexuality that involved answering an Internet or phone questionnaire? Check (✓) one.

    _____ I would be happy to participate.

    _____ I would be reluctant but probably agree to participate.

    _____ I would refuse to participate.

3. Would you feel differently if you were personally interviewed? Why?

Talk about Your Ideas

1. Compare your answers to the chart above. How much agreement and disagreement is there among your classmates? If your class had to design a sex education program, would compromise be possible?
2. Should scientists study human sexuality? If so, how?
3. Would members of your class agree to take part in a confidential study on sexual practices and attitudes? List the reasons why they would or would not.

For CNN video activities about the Kinsey controversy, turn to page 202.

CHAPTER

Cults:
Path to God or somewhere else?

a.

b.

c.

PREVIEW

Discuss these questions with your classmates.

1. Who are the people in the pictures above? Can you name any of them? What are they famous for?

2. In general, what are some *differences* between cults and mainstream religions?

3. What are some *similarities* between cults and mainstream religions?

4. Are there any well-known cults in your country? What are they? How do people feel about them?

(See next page for answers to Question 1.)

Preview photos depict a. Shoko Asahara, whose cult released poison gas in a Tokyo subway in 1995; b. Charles Manson, whose cult murdered actress Sharon Tate and others in 1970; and c. Marshall Herff Applewhite, whose cult committed mass suicide in 1997.

PART I

Predict

A. Skim the readings and make predictions.

1. Which reading . . .
   a. tells a story?
   b. gives definitions?
   c. cites scientific research?

2. Which writers . . .
   a. are trying to persuade readers?
   b. are trying to inform readers?

3. Predict the difficulty of each reading.
   a. Reading 1A

   very easy   pretty easy   difficult   very difficult

   b. Reading 1B

   very easy   pretty easy   difficult   very difficult

   c. Reading 2

   very easy   pretty easy   difficult   very difficult

B. Write a question that you think each reading will answer.

Reading 1A

_____

Reading 1B

_____

Reading 2

_____

Read It

Read the articles and look for the answers to your questions.

 READING 1A

> # Cult Versus Religion: What's the Difference?
>
> **It depends on who you talk to . . .**
>
> Mainstream religions have always viewed new religions with suspicion. Not infrequently, they say that new religions are heretical and socially dangerous. While the past fifty years has seen a growing acceptance of the principle of "universal human rights," in this same period there has also been even more opposition to new religions.
>
> The dictionary defines the term *cult* as "a system of religious beliefs or rituals." However, the general public often uses the term *cult* to describe any religious group they view as strange or dangerous. The word is most often used to refer to religious leaders or organizations that employ abusive, manipulative, or illegal control over their followers' lives.
>
> When anticult activists describe cults, they often make the following generalizations:
>
> - Cults are groups that often exploit members psychologically and/or financially through certain types of psychological manipulation, popularly called *mind control*;
> - Cults encourage excessive devotion or dedication to some person, idea, or thing;
> - Cults employ unethically manipulative techniques of persuasion and control;
> - Cults convince members to sacrifice their own welfare for the good of the group.
>
> Because the word *cult* has such negative connotations, most cultists do not use it. They describe themselves simply as followers of a new religion. They often point out that virtually every mainstream religion was once labeled a cult.

The Myth of Brainwashing

One of the main beliefs that the public holds about cults is that they *brainwash*, or use methods of thought control, on their followers. However, social psychologists who have studied brainwashing say that it does not exist. In an article titled *"What messages are behind today's cults?,"* Dr. Philip Zimbardo, professor of psychology at Stanford and former president of the American Psychology Association, claims that cults do not use strange or unusual methods of mind control. According to him, cultists use everyday strategies to influence their members. However, they use these strategies more intensely.

Cult leaders offer simple solutions to the increasingly complex world problems we all face daily. They offer the simple path to happiness, to success, to salvation by following their simple rules, simple group regimentation, and simple total lifestyle. Ultimately, each new member contributes to the power of the leader by trading his or her freedom for the illusion of security and reflected glory that group membership holds out.

The best evidence that brainwashing does not exist is that, despite years of work and unlimited money, no government organization has ever been able to design effective brainwashing techniques. Experiments in thought control by the CIA and the former KGB were all unsuccessful. Both groups tried many methods including drugs and electroshock but nothing worked. How is it possible that relatively uneducated cult leaders could succeed in a week or two where experts failed over years?

Statistics show that cult recruitment programs are relatively ineffective. For example, researcher Eileen Barker documents that out of 1,000 people persuaded by the Moonies (Unification Church) to attend one of their overnight programs in 1979, 90 percent had no further involvement. Only 8 percent joined for more than one week. Another indicator cults are not in control of their members' minds is the high turnover rate of members. Barker says that 50 percent of members leave during the first two years. Consequently, it seems clear that mind control is simply a product of the public's unreasonable fear of cults.

Source: Philip Zimbardo, "What messages are behind today's cults? Cults are coming. Are they crazy or bearing critical messages?" http://www.snc.edu/psych/korshavn/

Salvation on the World Wide Web

Cult Used the Internet to Spread Its Message

The members of the Heaven's Gate believed that Hale-Bopp, an unusually bright comet, was the sign that they were supposed to leave their earthly bodies and join a spacecraft traveling behind the comet. As a result, in March, 1997, all 39 members did just that. They committed suicide. They died in shifts, with some members helping others take a lethal cocktail of phenobarbital and vodka before drinking their own doses of the deadly mixture. Police found a strangely calm and orderly scene when they arrived on March 26.

The Heaven's Gate Cult was founded in the late 1970s by Marshall Applewhite and his companion, Bonnie Lu Nettles, who died in 1985. The two, who first called themselves Bo and Peep and later Ti and Do,[1] claimed to be space aliens. They told people that they were in contact with aliens from a heavenly kingdom. Their religion was a mix of eastern philosophy, Christianity, and astrology. Technology was also an important part of their belief system. All the members were web designers who used the Internet to recruit members. Potential cult members could read about Heaven's Gate on the Internet.

The joy is that our Older Member in the Evolutionary Level above human (the "Kingdom of Heaven") has made it clear to us that Hale-Bopp's approach is the "marker" we've been waiting for. Our 22 years of classroom here on planet Earth is finally coming to conclusion—"graduation" from the Human Evolutionary Level. We are happily prepared to leave "this world" and go with Ti's crew.

The Internet was just becoming popular at the time and many people did not really understand it. When people heard of the suicides, some worried that cultists had found an effective new way to spread their messages. Indeed, it worked for some. According to Wendy Gale Robinson of the Department of Religion at Duke University, post office worker and Internet addict Yvonne McCurdy-Hill left five children and all her worldly possessions to join the group. Others argue that the vast number of voices in cyberspace drowns out the cults. "There's between 30 to 40 million Web pages out there," argues Karen Coyle, a spokesperson for Computer Users for Social Responsibility. "They could have done just as well to . . . throw a message in a bottle."

[1]Bo Peep is the name of a nursery rhyme character. Ti and Do are the names of two notes in the musical scale—Do Re Mi Fa So La Ti Do.

Adapted from "One year later, Heaven's Gate suicide leaves only a faint trail" with permission. Copyright © 1998 CNN.

Reading Comprehension

Check Your Predictions

1. Look back at questions 1–3 in the Predict section. How accurate were your predictions?

Prediction	Not Accurate	Accurate
1a		
1b		
1c		
2a		
2b		
3a		
3b		
3c		

2. If you found the answers to your questions, what were they?

Reading 1A

_____

Reading 1B

_____

Reading 2

_____

Check the Facts

READING 1A

Write T for *true,* F for *false,* or NS for *not sure.*

_____ 1. The public believes that cults have rituals.

_____ 2. The public believes that cult members are free to leave whenever they want.

_____ 3. The public believes that cults are similar to mainstream religions.

_____ 4. The public believes that cults are dangerous.

_____ 5. The public believes that cult members do not have free will.

READING 1B

Check (✓) the questions you can answer after reading once. Then go back and look for the answers you are unsure of.

_____ 1. Who is Philip Zimbardo?

_____ 2. Does he believe that cults brainwash their followers? Why or why not?

_____ 3. How does Zimbardo think that cults influence their followers?

_____ 4. What two groups tried to find brainwashing techniques?

_____ 5. What kinds of techniques did they try?

_____ 6. Were they successful?

_____ 7. What two statistics does Eileen Barker use to show that cults do not use mind control?

READING 2

Check (✓) the questions you can answer after reading once. Then go back and look for the answers you are unsure of.

_____ 1. Why did the Heaven's Gate followers commit suicide?

_____ 2. Who started the cult?

_____ 3. What did the founders tell people?

_____ 4. How did they use the Internet?

_____ 5. Why were some people worried about the Internet?

_____ 6. Does Karen Coyle believe that cults can easily use the Internet to recruit new members? Why or why not?

_____ 7. What does "throw a message in a bottle" refer to?

Analyze

1. What would most people say are the main differences between cults and mainstream religions?

2. In what ways was the Heaven's Gate Cult similar to the public's conception of cults?

3. How does Zimbardo's work contradict the public's belief about cults?

Vocabulary Work

Guess Meaning from Context

1. Look for these words in the readings. Decide if they are necessary for understanding the authors' main points. Use these types of clues to guess their meanings:

   - world knowledge of cults and religions
   - world knowledge of psychology
   - logic

Word	Reading	Meaning
heretical	1A	_____
rituals	1A	_____
exploit	1A	_____
sacrifice	1A	_____
welfare	1A	_____
connotation	1A	_____
salvation	1B	_____
regimentation	1B	_____
illusion	1B	_____
suicide	2	_____
lethal	2	_____
cocktail	2	_____
phenobarbital	2	_____
astrology	2	_____

2. Writers often use cultural references that may be unknown to nonnative speakers. What do *KGB* and *CIA* refer to? If you don't know, can you guess what kind of organizations they were?

   KGB _____

   CIA _____

Guess Meaning from Related Words

1. Underline the common words in these compound words and phrases.
   Guess the words and phrases' meanings.

Word/Phrase	Reading	Meaning
brainwash	1B	_____
everyday	1B	_____
electroshock	1B	_____
turnover	1B	_____
drown out	2	_____
spokesperson	2	_____

2. Find other forms of these words in the readings.

Reading 1A

suspect	_____
accept	_____
oppose	_____
abuse	_____
manipulate	_____
excess	_____
dedicate	_____
persuade	_____

Reading 1B

intense	_____
increase	_____
relative	_____

Reading 2

earth	_____
dead	_____
cult	_____

3. Work in pairs. Put the words from Exercises 1 and 2 in the correct columns
   in the chart on the next page. Compare your work with another pair when
   you are done.

Noun (person)	Noun (thing)	Verb	Adjective	Adverb

4. Look at the meanings of these prefixes. Then look for the words in the readings that use them and guess their meanings.

Prefix	Meaning	Word(s)	Meaning
astro-	star	_____	_____
in-	not	_____	_____
		_____	_____
un-	not	_____	_____
		_____	_____
		_____	_____
		_____	_____
		_____	_____
		_____	_____
		_____	_____

Reading Skills

Understanding Appositives

As you recall, appositives are words or phrases that add information about a person or thing. They are often separated from the main word by commas.

Look back at Readings 1B and 2 and find appositives that give more information about these people.

Philip Zimbardo	_____
Hale-Bopp	_____
Bonnie Lu Nettles	_____
Yvonne McCurdy Hill	_____
Karen Coyle	_____

Discussion

1. Do you think that cults are dangerous? Why or why not?
2. Should the government try to eliminate cults such as Heaven's Gate? If so, how? If not, why not?
3. Could you ever imagine joining a cult?

PART II

This reading is more difficult than the articles in Part I. Read it for the main ideas. Do not worry if you cannot understand everything.

Read It

Read to find the answers to these questions.

1. When and where did cargo cults begin?
2. How did World War II increase the importance of cargo cults?
3. What happened at the end of the war?
4. What did the people on the island of Tana originally believe?
5. What happened when the soldiers arrived?
6. What did the people try to do after the soldiers left?

Cargo Cults

The term *cargo cult* refers to religions that began among primitive tribes-people on islands in the South Pacific. Cargo cults first began in the mid 1800s, but became much more common during and after World War II. During the war, soldiers brought huge amounts of goods or cargo to the islands. Much of this was totally beyond the experience of the primitive tribal people. Items such as clothing, canned food, tents, weapons, and electrical equipment arrived for the soldiers—and also the islanders, who acted as their guides and hosts.

When the war ended, the air bases were abandoned and no new cargo arrived. The tribes, upset at the change, made great efforts to make the goods reappear. The cultists believed that the foreigners had some special connection to their ancestors, who were the only beings powerful enough to deliver such riches. In an attempt to get more cargo, islanders carved headphones from wood and wore them while sitting in control towers. They waved the landing signals while standing on the airport runways. They lit signal fires and torches to attract planes. They even built life-size "airplanes" out of straw. Eventually, the Pacific cultists gave up. But, from time to time, the term *cargo cult* is used as an idiom to mean any group of people blindly following something that is obvious they do not comprehend.

The Cult of John Frum

Most cargo cults were short-lived. The longest lasting and most famous is the John Frum Cult on the island of Tana in Vanuatu (formerly called the New Hebrides). The members of this cult have been waiting over 40 years for the return of American soldiers. Long before the arrival of the soldiers, the islanders believed in a legend that a mighty god would come from the air and the sea to begin a time of peace and prosperity. Their legend also claimed that 50,000 warriors were waiting inside the volcano Mount Tukomeru to lead them into victory.

The arrival of American servicemen on the island during World War II strengthened the islanders' belief in the legend. John Frum emerged as the name of their messiah. Although there are no records of an American soldier with that name, the islanders created ceremonies to honor and worship their mythical savior. Islanders carved American warplanes and military artifacts, such as helmets and rifles, from bamboo to use as religious icons. In addition, the islanders marched in parades with "U.S.A." painted,

(Continued on next page)

carved, or tattooed on their chests and backs. Some of them burned their money, killed their cattle, and left their homes, awaiting the new life promised by the mysterious god.

When the last American soldiers left at the end of the war, the islanders predicted John Frum's return. The movement continued to grow and on February 15, 1957, an American flag was raised in Sulphur Bay to declare the religion of John Frum. It is on this date every year that John Frum Day is celebrated. Cultists believe that John Frum is waiting in the volcano Yasur with his warriors to deliver his cargo to the people of Tana. During the festivities, the elders march in an imitation army, a kind of military exercise mixed with traditional dancing. Some carry guns made of bamboo and wear American army memorabilia such as caps, T-shirts, and coats. They believe that their annual rituals will make the god John Frum come down from the volcano to deliver prosperity to all of the islanders.

Reprinted from "Cargo Cults." http://www.bbc.co.uk/dna/h2g2/A2267426, with permission. Copyright © 2004 BBC.

Vocabulary Work

Guess Words from Context

1. Do you need to understand all of these words to answer the prereading questions? Cross out (~~word~~) the words that you can ignore. <u>Underline</u> the words you know. (Circle) the words you need to guess.

primitive	runways	warriors	cattle
control towers	legend	tattooed	memorabilia
blindly	artifacts	bamboo	ancestors
carved	imitation	reappear	savior
festivities	abandoned	straw	mysterious
hosts	life-size	messiah	

2. Try to use the following kinds of clues to help you understand the words in Exercise 1. Remember, it is often necessary to put several clues together in order to make a good guess. Write each word under the clue that helped you understand its meaning.

It looks like a word I know and/or I understood the prefix or suffix.

_____

I used my knowledge of cults and religions

_____

I used my knowledge of primitive people.

_____

I used my knowledge of airplanes and armies.

_____

I used logic.

_____

The writer gave a definition or explanation.

_____

The writer gave an example.

_____

Reading Skills

Identifying Cohesive Elements

Writers do not repeat nouns too often. They use pronouns and other markers to refer to their topics. These are called **referents.** *Referents help the ideas of a sentence, paragraph, or essay stick closely together or to be cohesive.*

What are the referents of the following words and phrases?

1. Much of <u>this</u> was totally beyond the experience of the primitive tribal people.

2. . . . and also the islanders, who acted as <u>their</u> guides and hosts.

3. The cultists believed that the foreigners had some special connection to <u>their</u> ancestors, who were the only beings powerful enough to deliver <u>such riches</u>.

4. In an attempt to bring more cargo, islanders carved headphones from wood and wore <u>them</u> while sitting in control towers.

5. The members of <u>this cult</u> have been waiting over 40 years for the return of American soldiers.

6 Although there are no records of an American soldier with <u>that name,</u> . . .

7. Some of <u>them</u> burned their money, killed their cattle, and left their homes, awaiting the new life and world promised by <u>the mysterious god</u>.

Understanding Elision

Elision *is the omission of certain words that are "understood" by the reader.*

> Mark, [who was] happy to be home from school, helped his mother clean the house. Sally doesn't like cooking but [she] does it when she has to.

As a reader, you must be able to figure out what a writer has left out. The words in brackets are left out when using elision.

Complete these sentences with the missing words.

1. Cargo cults first began in the mid 1800s, but _____ became much more common during and after World War II.

2. They waved the landing signals while _____ standing on the airport runways.

3. *Cargo cult* is used as an idiom to mean any group of people _____ blindly following something that it is obvious they do not comprehend.

4. Some _____ carry guns made of bamboo and wear American army memorabilia such as caps, T-shirts, and coats.

Idea Exchange

Think about Your Ideas

1. What is your opinion of cults? Check (✓) where your opinion lies on this scale.

← ——————————————————————————— →

positive   neutral   negative

2. Circle the words and phrases that you think describe cults. Then use them to write a definition of a cult on the next page.

mainstream	ritual	security
excessive	heretical	illogical
salvation	unethical	family
structure	freedom	manipulative
opposition	beliefs	brainwash
dangerous	helpful	complex
persuasive	abusive	unreasonable
mind control	hopeful	support
simplistic		

A cult is _____

_____

_____

_____

_____

_____

_____

Talk about Your Ideas

Divide into groups according to your opinions of cults. Write a group definition of a cult. Share your definition with other groups. How are they the same? How are they different?

_____

_____

_____

_____

For CNN video activities about the Heaven's Gate cult, turn to page 203.

CHAPTER 14

Strange Brains:
Unlocking the Secrets

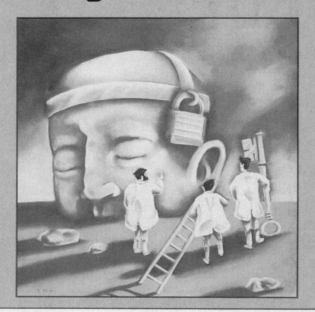

PREVIEW

A. Do you agree or disagree with these statements? Give each statement a number.

1	2	3	4	5
Strongly disagree		Not sure		Completely agree

1. I don't believe in psychiatry. _____
2. Many mental problems can be treated with medication. _____
3. You can get better advice from a friend than you can from a psychologist that you have to pay. _____
4. Talk therapy is helpful for many people. _____

5. People with strong family ties don't have mental problems. _____

6. People who are mentally ill are possessed by the devil. _____

7. They should close all mental institutions. _____

8. Mental illness cannot be cured. _____

9. Few people really need to go to psychologists. _____

10. Mental illness can be inherited. _____

B. Discuss your ideas with your classmates.

PART I

Predict

A. Skim the readings and make predictions.

1. Who are these people?

   a. Vladimir Nabokov _____

   b. Richard Cytowic _____

   c. Vilayanur Ramachandran _____

   d. Rudi Affolter _____

   e. Gregory Holmes _____

   f. Ellen G. White _____

   g. Daniel Giang _____

2. Predict the difficulty of each reading.

   a. Reading 1

       very easy   pretty easy   difficult   very difficult

   b. Reading 2

       very easy   pretty easy   difficult   very difficult

B. Write a question that you think each reading will answer.

Reading 1

_____

Reading 2

_____

Read It

Read the articles and look for answers to your questions.

READING 1

Ever Taste a Shape or Smell a Color?

Neurologist explores strange world of synesthesia.

ATLANTA, Georgia—Can you conceive of smelling a number, seeing a sound, tasting a color? Most people find all of these unimaginable. However, for a very small percentage of the population, such sensations are normal. These people have *synesthesia.* Synesthesia means "joined sensation." It is not voluntary. It is an automatic physical experience in which one sense sets off a perception in a different sense or senses. For example, a synesthete not only sees the color purple, but might "smell" it, or see it as a shape, too.

Synesthesia has a different impact on different people. For some, it is a disorder that makes their lives more difficult. In others, it is just an interesting phenonmenon. However, synesthesia is very rare. It occurs in about one in 25,000 individuals. Women are twice as likely to be synesthetic as men, and it also runs in families.

Famous Russian writer Vladimir Nabokov was a synesthete. When he was a child, he complained to his mother that

the colors on his wooden alphabet blocks were all wrong. The *A* was purple on the blocks, whereas, to him, *A* was blue. He thought, "How could anybody be so stupid to make this kind of mistake?" His mother understood because she had the same kind of synesthesia in which letters and numbers were colored.

Most synesthetes are surprised to discover as children that other people don't perceive the world in the same way. For example, a child makes some innocent comment like, "The music looks like a yellow rose." And his mother says, "Are you crazy?" As a result, the child learns to only talk about the same kinds of perceptions other people do. Sometimes they begin to doubt whether their perceptions are real.

But real they are. For some synesthetes, music is not just a sound. It's a visual fireworks. They often see visions in front of them on a little screen rather than in their mind's eye. Some say that if you want to understand it, see Walt Disney's *Fantasia,* an animated film with sections that attempt to visualize music.

Richard Cytowic, who has researched and written about synesthesia, says that synesthetic perceptions are very consistent over time. Experiments have shown that synesthetes will give exactly the same response over their whole lives. So that if the letter *C* is blue, or if a certain voice looks like a falling star, the perception will remain the same forever.

Cytowic believes that we are all born synesthetes but that most of us lose this ability as we mature. He believes a search to understand the condition will eventually lead to a new model of the mind.

Reprinted from "Synethesia" with permission. Broadcast by the Australian Broadcasting Corporation, Radio National, Health Report. Copyright © 1996.

God on the Brain

Controversial new research suggests that belief in God may not be totally a matter of free will. Science is discovering that there are differences in the brains of very religious people and others. How was this connection made? Dr. Vilayanur Ramachandran, a researcher at the University of California in San Diego, noticed that an unusual number of people with a disorder called temporal lobe epilepsy[1] had religious visions. In addition, many only experienced these visions after developing the condition. For example, Rudi Affolter was and still is a confirmed atheist. However, when he was

43, Affolter had a powerful religious vision which convinced him he had gone to hell. "I was told that I had gone there because I had not been a devout Christian, a believer in God. I was very depressed at the thought that I was going to remain there forever."

Dr. Ramachadran wanted to investigate so he set up an experiment to compare the brains of people with and without temporal lobe epilepsy. He decided to measure his patients' changes in skin resistance or galvanic skin response. (This is the same response that a lie detector measures.) What Ramachandran discovered was that when the temporal lobe patients were shown any type of religious images, there was a dramatic change in their skin resistance. This was the very first piece of clinical evidence that the body's response to religious symbols was linked to the temporal lobes of the brain. "What we suggested was that there are certain circuits within the temporal lobes which have been selectively activated in these patients and somehow the activity of these specific neural circuits makes them more prone to religious belief."

Scientists now believe famous religious figures in the past could also have suffered from the condition. For example, American neurologist Gregory Holmes studied the life of Ellen G. White, who was the founder of the Seventh-Day Adventist movement. Today, the movement is a thriving church with over 12 million members. During her life, White had hundreds of dramatic religious visions that helped to convince people to follow her. But Professor Holmes believes there may be another explanation for her visions.

Head Trauma

He learned that at the age of nine, Ellen suffered a severe blow to her head. As a result, she was semiconscious for several weeks. Following the accident, Ellen's personality changed dramatically. She began to develop personality traits such as paranoia, anger, dependence, religiosity, sadness, philosophical interest, and humorlessness. All of these traits are common in people with temporal lobe epilepsy. In addition, for the first time in her life, she began to have powerful religious visions. Holmes is convinced that the blow to Ellen's head caused her to develop temporal lobe epilepsy.

Dr. Daniel Giang, a neurologist as well as a member of Seventh-Day Adventist Church, disagrees. He points out that the visions started years after the accident. He goes on to say that "Ellen White's visions lasted from 15 minutes to three hours or more. She never apparently had any briefer visions—that's quite unusual for seizures."

(Continued on next page)

We will never know for sure whether Ellen White or any other religious figures in the past had the disorder, but scientists now believe the condition provides a powerful insight into revealing how the brain may influence religious experience.

[1]Epilepsy is a brain disorder. It occurs when the electrical signals in the brain are disrupted. This change in the brain leads to a seizure (SEE-zhur). Seizures can cause brief changes in a person's body movements, awareness, emotions, and senses, such as taste, smell, vision, or hearing.

Adapted from "God on the Brain," BBC News Online, with permission. Copyright © 2003 BBC.

Reading Comprehension

Check Your Predictions

1. Look back at questions 1 and 2 in the Predict section. How accurate were your predictions?

Prediction	Not Accurate	Accurate
1a		
1b		
1c		
1d		
1e		
1f		
1g		
2a		
2b		

2. If you found the answers to your questions, what were they?

Reading 1: _____

Reading 2: _____

Check the Facts

Check (✓) the questions you can answer after one reading. Then go back and look for the answers that you are unsure of.

READING 1

_____ 1. Describe synesthesia.

_____ 2. Out of 100,000 people, how many are likely to have synesthesia?

_____ 3. Are women or men more likely to have synesthesia?

_____ 4. What do some synesthetes see when they hear music?

_____ 5. Do synthesthetic perceptions change over time?

READING 2

_____ 1. Where are the temporal lobes?

_____ 2. Does Rudi Affolter believe in God?

_____ 3. What happened when he developed temporal lobe epilepsy?

_____ 4. How did Dr. Ramachadran research this condition?

_____ 5. Why does Dr. Holmes believe that Ellen G. White had temporal lobe epilepsy?

_____ 6. Does Dr. Giang agree? Why or why not?

Analyze

1. Compare the two conditions. Which one probably has a more negative effect on people's lives—synesthesia or temporal lobe epilepsy?

2. Find at least one argument in each article that is controversial and one that is proven.

Vocabulary Work

Guess Meaning from Context

Look for these words in the readings. Decide if they are necessary for understanding the authors' main points. Use these types of clues to guess their meanings:

- world knowledge of psychology
- world knowledge of religion
- logic
- an example
- a definition or a synonym

Word	Reading	Meaning
neurologist	1	_____
automatic	1	_____
sets off	1	_____
phenomenon	1	_____
consistent	1	_____
atheist	2	_____
galvanic skin response	2	_____
circuits	2	_____
neural	2	_____
prone	2	_____
founder	2	_____

thriving	2	_____
blow	2	_____
traits	2	_____
paranoia	2	_____
seizures	2	_____

Guess Meaning from Related Words

1. Look at these pairs of words and try to guess their meanings.

   mind's eye _____

   lie detector _____

2. Find other forms of these words in the readings.

   imagine _____

   volunteer _____

   synesthesia _____

   perceive _____

   religious _____

   humor _____

3. Work in pairs. Put the words from Exercises 1 and 2 in the correct columns. Compare your work with another pair when you are done.

Noun (person)	Noun (thing)	Verb	Adjective	Adverb

4. Look at the meanings of these prefixes. Then look for the words in the readings that use them and guess their meanings.

Prefix	Meaning	Word(s)	Meaning
dis-	not	_____	_____
un-	not	_____	_____

Reading Skills

Identifying Main Ideas and Supporting Details

1. Both articles have the same purpose. Is it to persuade, instruct, explain, or compare? How do you know?

2. Complete the chart below.

	Main ideas	Types of supporting details (statistics, examples, quotes, logic, citations, etc.)
Reading 1		
Reading 2		

Differentiating Fact from Opinion

1. Reading 1 only contains one opinion. What is it?

2. Look at Reading 2. Draw two lines under the facts you find. Circle the opinions.

3. What aspect of the article shows that the writer tried to give a balanced view of the controversy?

4. Read the statements below. How do they show the writer's opinion of the controversy?

    a. *Science is discovering that there are differences in the brains of very religious people and others. How was this connection made?*

    b. *Scientists now believe famous religious figures in the past could also have suffered from the condition.*

    c. *. . . but scientists now believe the condition provides a powerful insight into revealing how the brain may influence religious experience.*

Discussion

1. Would you like to be synesthetic? Why or why not?

2. Do you believe that a brain disorder could cause religious visions? Why or why not?

3. If a brain disorder can cause religious visions, does this mean that human brains are "wired" for religion and the disorder simply makes the brain malfunction?

PART II

This reading is more difficult than the articles in Part I. Read it for the main ideas. Do not worry if you cannot understand everything.

Read It

Read to find the answers to these questions.

1. What four things do Bush and Eldridge have in common?
2. What do people with MSBP do?
3. How do people with MSBP fool doctors?
4. What percentage of children who are abused die?
5. What do people with MSBP want?

 READING

Parenthood Betrayed: The Dilemma of Munchausen Syndrome by Proxy
by *Marc D. Feldman, M.D.*

Too Much in Common

Kathleen Bush and Yvonne Eldridge had a lot in common. First, both cared for children with extremely complex medical problems: Jennifer Bush suffered from constant intestinal problems, and Eldridge's two foster daughters had many ailments that left them weak and emaciated. Second, both Bush and Eldridge spent most of their time taking their sickly girls from doctor to doctor. Jennifer was hospitalized 200 times, and all three children had to undergo surgery to place feeding tubes into their stomachs. Third, both parents received the highest praise for their devotion to their little charges. Bush was praised by Hilary Clinton at a 1994 White House rally, while Eldridge was named national "Mother of the Year" in 1988 by First Lady Nancy Reagan.

Yet prosecutors later discovered that Kathleen Bush and Yvonne Eldridge also shared a dark secret. Bush and Eldridge were accused of having a strange psychiatric ailment called "Munchausen syndrome by proxy" that made them manufacture the girls' illnesses because of their own needs for attention and sympathy. Bush deliberately poisoned and infected her daughter; Eldridge starved her foster children and reported symptoms that never existed.

A Web of Deceit

The term *Munchausen syndrome by proxy* (MSBP) was coined around twenty years ago. Hundreds of cases have been reported since then. In most cases, a mother either claims that her child is sick, or she goes even further to actually make the child sick. This "devoted" parent then continually takes the child for medical treatment, always denying any knowledge of the origin of the problem—that is, herself. As a result, MSBP victims may undergo extraordinary numbers of lab tests, medications, and even surgical procedures that aren't really needed. For instance, by the age of eight, Jennifer Bush had had more than 40 operations, including the removal of much of her intestines. Other children are forced to spend almost every day of their lives in the hospital or at the doctor's office.

The lies that the caretaker tells can be supported by medical signs and symptoms that mislead the most skillful doctors. They are often excellent actors. For instance, the MSBP perpetrator might cause apnea, a cessation of breathing, by suffocating her child to the point of unconsciousness, then frantically rush to the hospital and display the limp child to the staff as the tears roll down her cheeks. She may secretly place a drop of blood in the child's urine, and then appear horrified at the lab results. Behind closed doors, she may scrub the child's skin with oven cleaner to cause a skin rash that lasts for months. Since it may take many years of illness for doctors to finally realize the truth, it is not surprising that 9 percent of the children who suffer this abuse die.

Struggling to Understand

Why would anyone do such a thing? Everyone who hears about MSBP asks the same question. Few other behaviors so severely challenge our concept of motherhood. Typically, it seems, the MSBP parent is on a misguided mission to feel special, to get attention from people—family, friends, and community—as a heroic caretaker. Others desire a relationship with doctors in which they get attention by defeating them through their carefully crafted deceptions. And virtually all have personality disorders that lead them to behave in odd and even destructive ways, especially when they feel under stress.

Protecting the Defenseless

When MSBP is suspected, health-care providers are required by law to report their concerns. Since MSBP can be deadly, law enforcement will usually step in to investigate while social service agencies focus on the highest priority of all—ensuring continued protection of the child.

Reprinted from "Parenthood Betrayed" with permission. Copyright © 1998 Marc D. Feldman.

Vocabulary Work

Guess Meaning from Context

1. Do you need to understand all of these words to answer the prereading questions? Cross out the words (~~word~~) that you can ignore. <u>Underline</u> the words you know. (Circle) the words you need to guess.

in common	intestinal	foster	prosecutors
emaciated	undergo	feeding tube	infected
psychiatric	ailment	poisoned	claims
starved	symptoms	cases	apnea
origin	extraordinary	frantically	limp
suffocating	unconsciousness	skin rash	motherhood
urine	scrub	destructive	priority
misguided	caretaker	weak	ensuring

2. Try to use the following kinds of clues to help you understand the words in Exercise 1. Remember, it is often necessary to put several clues together in order to make a good guess. Write the word under the clue that helped you understand its meaning.

It looks like a word I know and/or I understood the prefix or suffix.

_____

I used my knowledge of psychology.

_____

I used my knowledge of medicine.

_____

I used logic.

_____

The writer gave a definition or explanation.

_____

The writer gave an example.

_____

Reading Skills

Understanding Transition Words

What ideas from the reading do these transition words connect?

- first, second, third
- yet
- for instance
- since

Identifying Cohesive Elements

Go back to the reading and circle the referents of the <u>underlined</u> words and phrases.

1. Hundreds of cases have been reported since <u>then</u>.
2. <u>This "devoted" parent</u> then continually takes <u>the child</u> for medical treatment, always denying any knowledge of the origin of the problem—<u>that is</u>, herself.
3. <u>They</u> are often excellent actors.
4. . . . then frantically rush to the hospital and display <u>the limp child</u> to <u>the staff</u> as the tears roll down her cheeks.
5. <u>She</u> may secretly place a drop of blood in the child's urine, . . .
6. She may scrub <u>the child's</u> skin with oven cleaner to cause a skin rash that lasts for months.
7. Since <u>it</u> may take many years of illness for doctors to finally realize the truth, ...

Idea Exchange

Think about Your Ideas

Which traits do you think are the result of nature—that is, you were born a certain way? Which traits do you think are the result of nurture—that is, you were raised a certain way? Write *nature, nurture,* or *both.*

_____ intelligence

_____ talent (musical, artistic, etc.)

_____ physical abilities (sports)

_____ personality

_____ degree of personal satisfaction with life

_____ morality

_____ belief in God or a higher power

(Exercise continued on next page)

_____ personal taste (in your surroundings)

_____ patriotism

_____ altruism

_____ capacity for hard work

_____ self-confidence

_____ irrational fear (e.g., phobias such as fear of heights, fear of closed spaces, fear of flying)

Talk about Your Ideas

Discuss these questions with your class.

1. Some people believe that all of human behavior is simply the result of chemical processes in the brain that are beyond any individual's control. Do you believe that this is so? If you do, do you think that people are then responsible for their actions? Why or why not?

2. Psychiatrists now believe that many of the greatest artists and writers had serious mental problems. Vincent van Gogh cut off his own ear and eventually committed suicide. The great American writer Edgar Allen Poe died of alcohol abuse. We now have the ability to eradicate or lessen the effects of mental illness with medication. Do you think that people who suffer from mental illness are more likely to create great art? Do people who are mentally unbalanced have a better perspective on the human condition?

For CNN video activities about one mother's psychological illness called Munchausen by Proxy, turn to page 204.

APPENDIX: CNN Video Activities

CHAPTER 1 **Work from Home Scam**

Think about It

Answer and discuss these questions.

1. Have you ever been involved in a work-at-home business opportunity such as stuffing envelopes? Describe the business. Did you make money?
2. If you've never actually participated in a work-at-home business, have you seen advertisements for any that seem interesting? Describe it.

Understand It

Read the statements. Then watch the video once or twice. As you watch the video, listen for the answers to these questions. Circle the correct answers.

1. Project Biz Opp Flop is the largest business opportunity fraud _____ by the Federal Trade Commission (FTC).
   a. investigation   b. crackdown   c. action   d. putdown
2. Law enforcement has taken action against operations that have affected tens of thousands of consumers who have _____ more than 100 million dollars.
   a. earned   b. made   c. gained   d. lost
3. Some scams have yielded losses of 50 to 100 dollars; others have cost consumers their _____ .
   a. life savings   b. credit cards   c. bank accounts   d. their lives
4. The FTC has not _____ anyone who has gotten rich at these work-at-home opportunities.
   a. found   b. met   c. blamed   d. investigated
5. The FTC has set up _____ to educate consumers.
   a. an office   b. a hotline   c. an operation   d. a Web site

Discuss It

1. What do you think of the FTC's idea for a Web site to educate consumers?
2. After watching this video, what do you think about work-at-home opportunities?

Write about It

Your friend is thinking about doing a work-at-home business. Write an e-mail to a friend warning him or her about work-at-home scams. Include information that you learned from the video.

CHAPTER 2 DNA WILL SET YOU FREE

Think about It

Answer and discuss these questions.

1. What do you think are the biggest problems of the criminal justice system in the United States?
2. What is your opinion of capital punishment (the death penalty)?

Understand It

Before you watch the video, read the statements. Watch the video once or twice. As you watch the video, listen for the words that complete these sentences. Write the words from the box on the blanks.

cleared	imperfect	video taped	revolution
letters	free	death row	evidence

1. DNA evidence has set these men _____.
2. DNA testing has caused a _____ in the criminal justice system.
3. Peter Neufeld has 200 pending cases and 4,000 _____ asking for help.
4. DNA evidence _____ 13 prisoners on death row in Illinois.
5. The Illinois governor commuted the death sentences of all 166 _____ prisoners.
6. The U.S. justice system is _____.
7. Illinois now has a law saying that confessions have to be _____.
8. Now suspects are being excluded from further suspicion based on DNA _____.

Discuss It

1. Do you think people should be convicted of murder if there is no DNA evidence?
2. Do you think it was right for former Illinois Governor Ryan to commute the sentences of all prisoners on death row? Why or why not?

Write about It

Write an email to a friend about the video on DNA evidence. Include a brief summary of the video and your feelings about the topic in the email.

CHAPTER 3 A Surrogate's Story

Think about It

Answer and discuss these questions.

1. What do you think of surrogate mothers? Do you know anyone who's been a surrogate?
2. Do you think it's common or unusual for a surrogate to have more than one child for a couple?

Understand It

Read the statements. Then watch the video once or twice. According to the video, which statements are true and which statements are false? Write *T* for *True* and *F* for *False.*

_____ 1. Pam can't produce eggs.

_____ 2. A decade ago Pam wouldn't have been able to have a child.

_____ 3. Sam already has two children.

_____ 4. Sam was not able to get pregnant the first time.

_____ 5. Sam does not have easy pregnancies.

_____ 6. It's very common that surrogates have more than one baby for a couple.

_____ 7. The procedure involves stimulating Pam's and Sam's egg production.

_____ 8. Pam and Gary's embryos were created in a lab.

_____ 9. Three embryos were transplanted into Sam's uterus.

_____ 10. Sam got pregnant again.

Discuss It

1. Sam has said that she will keep trying until she gets pregnant again with Pam and Gary's baby. Do you think this will happen? Why or why not?
2. Some religious leaders have come out strongly against in vitro-fertilization. Do you know the arguments against in vitro? Do you agree or disagree?

Write about It

Take a position. Are you for or against fertility treatments that involve surrogate mothers and in vitro fertilization? Explain your reasons.

CHAPTER 4 Gambling Addiction: Chasing the big win

Think about It

Answer and discuss these questions.

1. Do you ever gamble? What games do you play? How often do you play? What's the largest amount of money you've won or lost?
2. Does anyone you know have a gambling problem?

Understand It

Read the statements. Then watch the video once or twice. Answer the questions based on the information in the video.

1. What is Arnie?

    _____

2. What does Arnie do now?

    _____

3. What did Arnie wish he had enough guts to do?

    _____

4. According to Dr. Yamins, what can't a compulsive gambler do?

    _____

5. Why does Dr. Yamins call gambling an invisible addiction?

    _____

6. What drives the compulsion to gamble?

    _____

7. What did Arnie do every day of his life?

    _____

8. If addiction to gambling is an illness, why don't insurance companies cover treatment for it?

    _____

Discuss It

1. If gambling is such a large problem in the United States, should government allow and promote (e.g., lotteries) gambling?
2. Do you view compulsive gambling as a true addiction? Do you think insurance companies should cover treatment for compulsive gambling?

Write about It

Experts are saying that gambling is getting to be a problem with children and adolescents. What would you do if you saw your child or a young relative becoming involved in betting on sports games at school or playing poker for money with friends?

CHAPTER 5 · A DEAF FOOTBALL TEAM

Think about It

Answer and discuss these questions.

1. Have you ever gone to a sports event where athletes with disabilities were involved? What were your impressions?
2. Do you think athletes with disabilities can compete with athletes who don't have disabilities? Why or why not?

Understand it

Read the statements. Then watch the video once or twice. According to the video, which statements are true and which statements are false? Write *T* for *True* and *F* for *False*.

_____ 1. For the first time in the school's history the football team is in the league championship.

_____ 2. They want to be known as football players who are deaf.

_____ 3. Coach Len Gonzales knows that the other teams are too strong for them.

_____ 4. Coaches communicate by yelling very loud.

_____ 5. The opposing teams regularly underestimate the team from Riverside.

_____ 6. The team asks for several changes in the rules to compensate for their deafness.

_____ 7. The players won the play-off.

Discuss It

1. After viewing this video have your opinions changed or remained the same about athletes with disabilities? Explain.
2. What does William Albright, one of the players from Riverside, hope that his team will gain during this football season? Do you think they'll get it? Why or why not?

Write about It

Write a fan letter to the Riverside football team.

CHAPTER 6 father's double life

Think about It

Answer and discuss these questions.

1. Have you ever learned something shocking about someone that you thought you knew well?
2. What is a "double life?"

Understand It

Read the statements. Then watch the video once or twice. Answer the questions based on the information in the video.

1. Who was Jean Ann Cone?

   _____

2. How did she die?

   _____

3. Who was Douglas Cone?

   _____

4. Who was Donald Carlson?

   _____

5. Who was Hillary Carlson?

   _____

6. Did Jean Ann Cone and Hillary Carlson know each other?

   _____

7. What happened after Jean Ann Cone died?

   _____

8. How did friends and family find out that something was wrong?

   _____

9. Who knew about the double life?

   _____

Discuss It

1. How do you think it's possible that a man lead a double life in two households just 20 miles apart from each other?
2. Do you think Jean Ann Cone knew about her husband's other family? Explain.

Write about It

Pretend you're a journalist for a Tampa newspaper. Write down five to eight questions you'd like to ask Douglas Cone.

CHAPTER 7   Little Black Book Revealed

Think about It

Answer and discuss these questions.

1. What would you do if you heard on the news that a brothel was just discovered in your town?
2. Would you want to know who the clients were at the brothel?

Understand It

Read the statements. Then watch the video once or twice. As you watch the video listen for the answers to these questions. Check (✓) the correct answers.

1. Documents, video tapes, pornographic material taken from a local brothel were being made available for _____ .
   _____ a. the police to see   _____ c. lawyers to see
   _____ b. the judge to see   _____ d. the public to see
2. Angelika Potter ran a thriving prostitution _____ .
   _____ a. business   _____ c. investigation
   _____ b. hotline   _____ d. room
3. The brothel's owner received _____
   _____ a. a long jail sentence _____ c. a light punishment
   _____ b. no punishment   _____ d. ten to twenty years
4. The media became suspicious and wanted _____ to release the documents.
   _____ a. the brothel   _____ c. the judge
   _____ b. the police   _____ d. the mayor's office
5. Now anyone can look at the lists of clients and other information in

   _____
   _____ a. City Hall   _____ c. the newspaper
   _____ b. the courtroom   _____ d. the brothel

Discuss It

1. Do you think the punishment the brothel's owner received was fair? Why or why not?
2. Do you think the judge was right in forcing the mayor's office to make the documents available for the public to view? Why or why not?

Write about It

Would you go to City Hall to look at the list of clients or any of the materials? Why or why not?

CHAPTER 8 System Failure: Cheating in school

Think about It

Answer and discuss these questions.

1. Have you ever cheated?
2. How did you feel when you cheated? How do you feel about it now?
3. Is cheating common in your native country? Is there shame attached to cheating? Why or why not?

Understand It

Before you watch the video, read the statements. Watch the video once or twice. As you watch the video, listen for the words that complete these sentences. Write the words from the box on the blanks.

three quarters	plagiarized	honor	cutting corners
pressure	survive	submit	rampant

1. Many students feel that cheating is just a way to _____ in high school.
2. Alice Newhall feels that _____ will save you time and energy.
3. High school cheating is _____.
4. A survey of 4500 students found that _____ of them are engaged in serious cheating.
5. More than half have _____ work off the Internet.
6. Teachers now _____ students' work to an online company to check for plagiarism.
7. Students feel driven by the tremendous _____ to excel and compete for colleges.
8. Mike Denny feels that _____ is lacking in a large part of society.

Discuss It

1. Why do you think students may be cheating more than their parents did? Explain.
2. Compare Alice Newhall and Mike Denny and their views on cheating. How are they similar? How are they different? Do you feel more like Alice or more like Mike?

Write about It

If you were the school principal and found that three quarters of your students had engaged in "serious cheating" what would you do to change things?

CHAPTER 9 Debating Gender Differences

Think about It

Answer and discuss these questions.

1. Do you believe that women and men have the same abilities in general?
2. Why do you think that in the United States there aren't as many women scientists at the top of their fields as there are men scientists?
3. Talk about women in your native country or culture. Are there many women in science, engineering, and mathematics?

Understand it

Before you watch the video, read the statements. Watch the video once or twice. As you watch the video, listen to the comments made by Ms. Spillar and Ms. Pfotenhauer. What did they say? Check (✓) the correct column.

Views	Katherine Spillar	Nancy Pfotenhauer
1. Harvard President Summer is sexist.	_____	_____
2. President Summer is being punished for telling the truth.	_____	_____
3. Men have superiority is some areas and women in others.	_____	_____
4. Women are equal to men in all areas.	_____	_____
5. Women are discriminated against in the workplace.	_____	_____
6. Women make different career choices.	_____	_____
7. Girls aren't encouraged to achieve the most they can.	_____	_____
8. Women shouldn't present themselves as victims.	_____	_____

Discuss It

1. Do you think there are two sides to this debate? Talk about the points from each side of the debate that make sense to you.
2. Do you agree with the statement from the video that "society benefits from the debate sparked by one speech, by one Ivy League president?" Why or why not?

Write about It

Using the points you noted down in activity 1 above, write a paragraph about equality in the work force.

CHAPTER 10 IMMIGRATION IN MIDDLE AMERICA

Think about It

Think about and discuss these questions.

1. Are there not enough, just enough, or too many immigrants coming to the U.S. every year?
2. What are some of the discussions taking place about immigration in this country? Who do you think is happy or unhappy about U.S. immigration policy?

Understand It

Before you watch the video, read the statements. Watch the video once or twice. As you watch the video, listen for the words that complete these sentences. Write the words from the box on the blanks.

identity	annually	closed	taxes	exploding
illegal	languages	Vietnamese	Immigrants	taking care

1. Children in Garfield Elementary School speak 18 different
   _____.
2. The immigrant population in middle America is
   _____—in Missouri alone it's up by 81% in the
   1990s.
3. _____ have made this the richest, freest countries
   in world history.
4. The Federation for American Immigration Reform says the government lets too
   many legal immigrants in, and does not keep enough
   _____ ones out.
5. Some Americans feel they're going to lose their
   _____ as Americans.
6. _____ are going to be higher to pay for services
   immigrants need.
7. Now 800,000 legal immigrants arrive _____.
8. The _____ community in Missouri have strong
   churches, businesses, and families.
9. Some children of immigrants think that U.S. immigration policy should be
   more _____.
10. _____ of children like Saib and their families is
    what America is all about.

Discuss It

1. Discuss the people in the video. (the school principal, Eric Ruiz, the program director, the FAIR members, Nhuoun and Doan Tran, the Vietnamese girl) Who is pro immigration? Who is against current immigration policies? How do you know?

(Continued on next page.)

2. The title and topic of this video selection is Immigration in Middle America. What is middle America? How does immigration affect middle America? Do you think people in middle America might have very different views on immigration than people from other sectors of the country? Why or why not?

Write about It

If you could make any changes to immigration policy in the U.S., what would they be?

(CHAPTER 11) MADE IN THE USA

Think about It

Answer and discuss these questions.

Do you recognize these brand names: RCA, Holiday Inn, Universal Studios, the Seattle Mariners, Skippy Peanut Butter? What country are these brands from?

Understand It

Read the statements. Then watch the video once or twice. According to the video, which statements are true and which statements are false? Write *T* for *True* and *F* for *False.*

_____ 1. When foreign firms take over U.S. firms, jobs are usually doubled in the United States.

_____ 2. Japanese automakers build many vehicles in the United States.

_____ 3. Data shows that after 5-10 years as many jobs are created as were lost in the takeover.

_____ 4. Americans are just as opposed to buying Japanese products as they were in the 1980s.

_____ 5. The American Heritage Dictionary is published by a French company.

Discuss It

Companies from countries who complain about American cultural imperialism own many American brands. What do you think about this?

Write about It

Write a brief description of five to ten American brand products that you buy or use regularly. Then try to find out if these products are actually produced by American companies or by companies from other countries.

CHAPTER 12 Kinsey Controversy

Think about It

Answer and discuss these questions.

1. Do people from your native country or culture talk more or less openly about sex than Americans?
2. What does the 'sexual revolution' mean to you? Do you think it's been good or bad for society?

Understand It

Before you watch the video, read the statements below. Watch the video once or twice. As you watch the video listen for the words that complete these sentences. Write the words from the box on the blanks.

revolution	average	disputed	culture
talk	controversial	fraud	casual

1. Now a _____ new movie explores the life of this radical researcher.
2. His findings are still _____, especially by conservatives.
3. Kinsey may have died in 1956, but his cold dead hand is still on the throttle of the sexual _____ and is still harming lives.
4. Look at how society has promoted _____ sex and what the results have been.
5. He relied on a disproportionate number of interviews with prisoners, homosexuals, and child molesters to develop his picture of _____ sexual practices.
6. His work was a _____, based on faulty numbers and cooked books.
7. He changed American _____ completely.
8. Alfred Kinsey certainly got one thing right: America was ready to _____ about sex, and that conversation continues.

Discuss It

1. Critics claim that Kinsey's research is faulty. Does this change the sexual revolution that he started?
2. Is there a person in your native country who has encouraged society to be more open about sex?

Write about It

Write about what you disapprove of or what you like about attitudes towards sex in American society.

CHAPTER 13 One Cult's Trip: To heaven?

Think about It

Answer and discuss these questions.

1. Do you know anyone who's ever belonged to a cult?
2. What famous cults do you know of? What are/were they famous for?

Understand It

Read the statements. Then watch the video once or twice. Answer the questions or complete the sentences based on the information in the video.

1. What were the names of Heaven's Gate founders?

   _____

2. What things were forbidden if you were a member?

   _____

3. How would they get to heaven?

   _____

4. One of the dead cult members was the brother of an actress. What TV show did she act in?

   _____

5. Some of the cult members wrote a _____ .
6. How long after the interview with the member in 1994, did the followers of Heaven's Gate take their lives? _____
7. How many members died? _____
8. Did the leader of Heaven's Gate also commit suicide? _____

Discuss It

The sister of one of the dead members said, "my brother was a highly intelligent and a beautifully gentle man. He made his choices, and we respect those choices." Do you respect his choices? Discuss her statement.

Write about It

Write about how you would react if a loved-one decided to join a cult such as Heaven's Gate.

CHAPTER 14 Mother's Dangerous Love

Think about It

Answer and discuss these questions.

What do you know about Munchausen's Syndrome by Proxy?

Understand It

Read the statements. Then watch the video once or twice. Match the sentences based on the information from the video.

_____ 1. She was named

_____ 2. Eldridge now faces charges

_____ 3. Kelly Hargreaves helped California

_____ 4. Kathy Bush deliberately sickened

_____ 5. Kathy Bush told the court

_____ 6. Jennifer has been

_____ a. take away Eldgridge's foster care license.

_____ b. to the hospital 200 times and has had 40 surgeries

_____ c. she's innocent.

_____ d. Mother of the Year in 1998.

_____ e. her nine-year-old daughter, Jennifer.

_____ f. of deliberately harming the children she cared for.

Discuss It

How is it possible that no one, not even doctors and other hospital staff, noticed the abuse that was going on until it was too late?

Write about It

Eldgridge and Bush, who suffer from a mental disorder known as Munchausen's Syndrome by Proxy, received national attention: first for appearing to be heroic mothers and then for the crimes they committed. So many good mothers get little credit for doing a great job. Write about a mother—such as your own or someone else's—that you think deserves the real positive attention of the public.